Contents

Introduction

BY PHIL PERKINS

So far in AA309 you have studied Rome, Italy, Greece, Asia Minor and Britain. In this block you will be studying a new part of the Roman empire, Africa. In the Roman world Africa formed the southern shores of the *Mare Nostrum* ('Our Sea' – the Mediterranean) around which the provinces of the empire were distributed. Africa was close to Italy and only a few days' sailing from Rome. Africa became a wealthy and influential part of the empire (in contrast to Britain), and an African, Septimius Severus, became emperor in AD 193. It did, however, have a history which set it apart from the Greek-speaking east and Italy for it was the homeland of the Carthaginians, the most significant rivals of Rome until the second century BC.

In this block you will be using skills you have learned in earlier blocks to investigate the art, archaeology, history and literature of Roman Africa. In some parts you will be practising familiar skills and in others you will be developing new ones. Our aims in the block are that you should:

- practise identification of 'indigenous' identity and culture;

- practise identification of 'Roman' identity and culture;

- study the development of a Romano-African culture;

- develop skills of modelling cultural development;

- consider the validity of making value judgements about cultural traits;

- develop a critical framework for the understanding of cultural history (whose point of view? African or Roman? colonized or colonial?); and

- practise a critical approach to cultural history written from a colonial viewpoint.

By the end of the block we hope you will have learned some new ways of looking at the Roman empire.

The block is divided into four parts. Part One begins with an introduction to North Africa that involves reading a background to the history and archaeology of Africa in Wells and Goodman. It moves on to a detailed investigation of a city in Africa. You will watch the video sequence 'Exploring Thugga' in video cassette 3, and undertake exercises identifying Roman and indigenous elements in the city. We then investigate Roman and indigenous cultural elements in the archaeology of Africa; here you will watch two brief video sequences on mosaics, continue your study of the 'Exploring Thugga' video, and view again 'Culture and identity in the houses of the Roman élite' from video cassette 1. Part Two explores literary and historical characterizations of Africans and Africa through extracts from Virgil, Sallust, Livy, Silius Italicus and Lucan. You will also read Essay Ten, 'The language of dissent', in *Experiencing Rome*. Part Three considers positive and negative aspects of Romano-African history, literature and art. It draws upon a range of evidence from Tacitus to the video sequence 'Economic power and exchange: Africa and Rome', Lewis and Reinhold and an extract from Apuleius; you will also re-read part of Essay Seven. In the final part you will look at how the history of Roman Africa has been written and its relationship to more recent history. You will study the views of a modern archaeologist, David Mattingly, by reading one of his articles in the Offprints Book and listening to an interview with him on audio cassette 4.

Part One: Roman, African, Romano-African or Afro-Roman?

BY PHIL PERKINS

1.1 Background

First of all you need to get a grounding in the history and geography of North Africa. Before reading in the set books by Goodman and Wells (which should take up to one hour), it is worth clarifying a few terms you will encounter in this block.

Phoenician: used to describe people and culture from Phoenicia – modern Lebanon and northern Israel. According to tradition the city of Carthage, the provincial capital of Roman Africa, was founded by settlers from Phoenicia in *c.* 814 BC led by queen Dido. Archaeological investigations have identified Phoenician culture in north-eastern parts of modern Tunisia from around this period, though there is no proof of Dido's existence.

Punic: derived from the Latin word for Phoenician but used to denote the people and their culture who lived in and around Carthage and northern Tunisia. Rome had three famous wars with these people: the 'Punic Wars'. In the first the Romans took Sicily; the second was fought against Hannibal and only narrowly won, and the third led to the destruction of Carthage and the Punic state in 146 BC. Punic civilization was a mixture of elements from Phoenicia and North Africa. Punic influence spread through North Africa, Spain, Sardinia and western Sicily.

Africa: strictly, this was used for the province of Africa, approximately modern Tunisia. It is largely used in that sense in this block, but occasionally it is used to indicate the wider area of the southern shore of the Mediterranean, excluding Egypt – what is now known as North Africa or the Maghreb. Though nowadays the term is used for the whole of the continent of Africa, it is not used to indicate the whole continent in this block.

Berber: a medieval and modern term for the tribal people who live in the interior of Tunisia and Algeria. It is also often used for peoples who lived there in earlier times.

To gain an overview of Roman Africa and become familiar with its history and geography, please read pages 276–84 of Goodman for a traditional historical account of Africa and take notes on the most important points. Next read Wells (pp.148–9 and 224–33) for further discussion of cities and an account of economic production.

This reading gives you an essential background, and you will return to some of the issues raised by them later in the block. Throughout this block we will concentrate on the province of Africa Proconsularis and its western neighbour, Numidia.

1.2   Exploring a Romano-African city: Thugga

The ancient city of Thugga is often known by its modern name, Dougga. In this block we will be using the ancient name, Thugga. In this section you will watch a video sequence taking occasional notes: it should form about an hour of study time. The next section follows on from the video and introduces further evidence from Thugga.

As you watch think about how the city compares with other cities you have encountered in the course so far: put it in the range you have studied from Rome to Pompeii, Ostia, Aosta, Athens, Ephesus, Colchester and Verulamium. Look out for how the buildings and streets are arranged, for familiar buildings such as temples or arches, for architectural decoration and also the language of the inscriptions. As well as the familiar, do look out for things that seem different. You will find it useful to refer to the plan of Thugga (Plate 5.1 in the Illustrations Book) as you watch the video. Use the pause button and jot down some notes: the next exercise is a detailed examination of the buildings in the city. Now watch the first video sequence in video cassette 3, 'Exploring Thugga' (t.c.00:03–23.14).

1.3   Investigating Roman and indigenous cultural elements in the archaeology of Africa

In this section you will be looking in more detail at the city of Thugga and working with the video and further evidence. This study of a city will then broaden out to consider other forms of material and visual evidence from different parts of Africa, for which you will need the Illustrations Book; you will also watch more video sequences. This section focuses upon one aspect of Romano-African culture: the interplay between Roman culture and indigenous African culture. This theme is one of a range of 'binary oppositions' which may be set up as a vehicle for investigating this part of the Roman empire. Other approaches could take the opposition of 'soldier' and 'civilian' (a theme investigated in Block Four) or 'emperor' and 'subject' (as in Blocks One and Two) or 'pastoralist' and 'agriculturalist' or 'desert' and 'sown' areas, using these as avenues of approach to the study of Africa. In Block Three you studied the meeting of Greek and Roman culture; here you will be investigating another meeting of cultures: African and Roman. In contrast to the Greek, African culture has left none of its own literature, and its achievements have not been as highly valued as Greek culture in the subsequent centuries. Because of this your study will start with material remains and monuments and only later move on to literature.

The first task is to try to tease out what can be seen as African characteristics in Roman Africa. To do this you will now be working in more detail on the city of Thugga. Thugga lies near the eastern boundaries of Numidia, which was an independent kingdom until 46 BC when it was annexed and became part of the Roman provinces of Africa and Numidia. The kingdom had urban centres such as Thugga, Bulla Regia and Simitthus, and was open to influences from the wider Mediterranean world. There was also a developed culture which had been exposed to Hellenistic influences. A good example of this is the Punic royal funerary monument at Thugga, which combines Punic and Hellenistic features, as you have seen on the video (see Figures 5.1 and 5.2). When Numidia became a part of the Roman empire, we might assume that Roman cultural influence would have become more pronounced and that perhaps a Roman identity might begin to emerge. But how might this be identified, and what kinds of things should we look for? Is it possible to see a distinct Roman culture and identity which might be compared and contrasted with a Numidian, or more generally an African, culture and identity? In the following sections of the block you will be looking for Roman and African identities and exploring the insights this can provide.

Exercise

Using the skills you have developed so far in the course, your knowledge of the parts of the Roman world you have studied, and what you have seen in the 'Exploring Thugga' video, in the following list of features (p.11) mark those which you think can be described as Roman in inspiration and which African or at least non-Roman. Also write a few words giving reasons for your choice. In some cases you may come to the opinion that some elements are both Roman and African; if so mark both boxes. You may like to watch 'Exploring Thugga' again to help you answer the questions, pausing the video at suitable points.

Figure 5.1   *Tomb of Ateban, son of Ypmatat (Punic mausoleum), early second century* BC, *Thugga. (Photo: P. Perkins)*

Figure 5.2 *The Punic mausoleum in Thugga before reconstruction in 1908–10. The reconstruction (as seen in Figure 5.1) was based on drawings made before partial demolition in 1842. DAI neg. no.55.1314. (Photo: Moscioni/German Archaeological Institute, Rome)*

Feature	Roman?	African?	Reason
City walls			
Street plan			
Temple of Mercury			
Temple of Augustan Piety			
Capitol			
Forum			
Theatre			
Political organization			
Arch of Alexander Severus			
Temple of Caelestis			
Temple of Saturn			
Saturn the god			
Circus			
Baths			
Construction techniques			
People			
Language			

Discussion

To answer the questions thoroughly would require detailed definitions of what was African and what was Roman, but even with such definitions the questions would not be easy to answer definitively and there is some subjectivity involved in the identifications. My answers (below) may differ slightly from yours. If they do, have a look at the reasons you and I have given and see if they explain why our opinions differ.

Feature	Roman?	African?	Reason
City walls	✗	✓	These don't surround the whole Roman city and they pre-date most of it, so they are African, even if their construction is not very different to Roman walls.
Street plan	✗	✓	The street plan is not like a regular Roman city grid as, for example, in Aosta or parts of Pompeii.
Temple of Mercury	✓	✓	The god is Roman but the building doesn't look much like a typical Roman temple.
Temple of Augustan Piety	✓	✓	The temple is to a Roman imperial cult, even if the building doesn't look like a typical Roman temple.
Capitol	✓	✗	It is typical of Roman cities, e.g. Pompeii or Ostia, and mimics the temple of Jupiter on the Capitoline hill in Rome, even if it has a different relationship to the forum.
Forum	✓	✗	It is the typical centre of a Roman city, an open square with columns around it.
Theatre	✓	✗	The theatre is Roman in style, similar to those at Pompeii, Ostia and elsewhere.

Feature	Roman?	African?	Reason
Political organization	✓	✓	The city seems to be divided into a *pagus* and a *civitas*: these are both Roman terms (and so it is a Roman element) but it is not typical of a Roman city where the *ordo* of decurions was the governing body (and so it may be African).
Arch of Alexander Severus	✓	✗	The arch is a typical Roman monument to commemorate a triumph or other honour.
Temple of Caelestis	✓	✓	The goddess is not originally Roman and the whole building doesn't look much like a typical Roman temple enclosure; nevertheless the actual temple has a podium and columns much like a Roman temple.
Temple of Saturn	✓	✓	The form of the temple is not like a typical Roman temple so perhaps it is African, even though there was a Roman Saturn.
Saturn the god	✓	✓	He (and his name) is originally Roman, but he took over the attributes of the pre-Roman god Baal in Africa, so he can be called African.
Circus	✓	✗	This is Roman because it repeats the form of the Circus Maximus race-track in Rome and other chariot race-tracks elsewhere.
Baths	✓	✗	The baths are similar to bath buildings in Rome and elsewhere.
Construction techniques	✗	✓	Most of the walls are not built in typical Roman styles of masonry.
People	✓	✓	They have both Roman and non-Roman names.
Language	✓	✗	Latin seems to be the language used in inscriptions, but we don't know what was spoken in every-day conversations.

The point of this exercise is to make you focus upon what can be conceived of as Roman and to think about whether or not some of the things you have met so far in Africa are familiar because you have already encountered similar things in Rome or elsewhere in the empire. Some of the cases above are fairly clear cut. Something like a capitol is obviously typical of Roman cities. Its precise form may vary (indeed at Thugga the temple is set side on rather than end on to the forum), but the configuration of a high temple with steps up the front and classical columns supporting a pediment with a *cella* behind (as the temple of Portunus in Rome studied in Block Two) dominating a forum fits the typical Roman model, as at Ostia or Pompeii. And we can get this far even before reading the dedication to the Capitoline Triad in the inscription above the door. Similar means can be used to suggest that the forum, theatre, circus, baths, and arch display features that we can recognize as distinctively Roman.

Other features, such as the temples of Saturn or Mercury, are harder to define as Roman: they may well use the same kinds of architecture but the ground plan is different, being like a rectangular courtyard or peristyle with three chambers set across a short end (see Plate 5.2). This is unlike the typical Roman temple: a building in an enclosure on a high podium with steps up the front and columns and a pediment on the façade. Perhaps it is a typically African form of temple because we have not encountered it in any of the other provinces studied so far. Indeed this style of temple has only ever been found in Africa, Mauretania and in the previously Punic Sardinia, and it does seem to be typical of African temples.

We can use the experience we have gained of looking at Roman buildings to see that the construction techniques are different; they employ a style known as *opus Africanum* (literally 'African work') that is characteristic of North Africa with origins that pre-date the Roman conquest. With this construction technique the wall is built incorporating vertical blocks of squared stones (orthostats), and the spaces between are filled with smaller blocks. Buildings you have seen elsewhere are built using different masonry techniques: brick-faced concrete (common in Ostia), small diamonds (common in Pompeii), small blocks of stone or larger squared blocks, for example.

We can also observe that the political organization and some of the names of the people are different to those we have previously encountered (see Figure 5.3 and p.22). We can begin to suspect that these differences may be related to something we might be able

Figure 5.3 *Inscription from the temple of Mercury naming the donors, Q. Pacuvius Saturus F.L. and Nahania Victoria, mid second century* AD, *Thugga. (Photo: P. Perkins)*

to identify as an African cultural identity and cultural expression, which we might contrast with a Roman identity and culture.

If, then, we can perceive different influences that we may call African and Roman (we must remember these terms are a shorthand for complex cultures that are not monolithic or clearly defined), we may also consider what may have happened when these two 'cultures' met in Africa following the political conquest of the region.

Modelling cultural interaction

To study this mixing of cultures in a systematic way I would like to propose four models of cultural interaction which might provide a framework for scenarios of what could have happened when the Roman met the African. First, it is worth briefly explaining what is meant by 'model' here. 'Model' is used to mean an explanation of a process of change. Once a model has been suggested, it can be held up for examination. If it is found not to fit the evidence or to explain observations, it may be discarded; if it does fit the evidence, it may help to build an understanding of the past. The theoretical models proposed here suggest what might have happened when two cultures – African and Roman – interacted. This is a new approach to interpretation and understanding which you have not yet met in this course. In Block Four you read Rick Jones ('Cultural change in Roman Britain', offprint 4.1) suggesting a strategy for interpreting evidence which involved observation (of his 'cultural forms') and contextualization (in his case focusing on the 'economic base') and interpretation (in his case focusing on 'social structure'). You have seen in Block Four how this can be applied to the study and interpretation of a sculptural relief – the Britannia and Claudius encounter from Aphrodisias (Plate 4.4). His schema is useful in its clarity, but it is not precise upon how the third stage is achieved. Jones has the interpretation phase of this process as a series of 'inferences drawn' from observation and contextualization, but provides little guidance on how this might be done. In the offprint the section on religion shows how another discipline, in this case anthropology, can be used as an aid to interpreting contextualized evidence. Jones acknowledges in his conclusion that there is a problem connecting evidence with hypotheses about social structure. The construction and consideration of theoretical models is one way of tackling this problem. From our observed and contextualized evidence we can construct models exploring various ways that this evidence may be interpreted. These models can then be used to reassess the evidence and so help both to frame questions about that evidence and to assess the appropriateness of the interpretation.

So in the case of Africa we can construct models of what might have been the result of the interaction of African and Roman cultural forms:

1   African meeting Roman leads to Roman dominance and an end of African traits: this may be called *assimilation.*

2   African meeting Roman leads to African traits continuing to dominate and Roman traits failing to become established, which amounts to *rejection.*

3   African meeting Roman leads to African persistence and no evidence of Roman traits dominating, in effect a *separation* of cultures.

4   African meeting Roman leads to Afro-Roman cultural mixing, which may be termed *fusion.*

These four models are gross simplifications, but I would like to comment upon each in turn and suggest some areas in the cultural, historical and archaeological record where we might hope to find indications of one or other of the models being fulfilled. The rest of the section will introduce some new forms of evidence, and you will be invited to consider how they compare to each of the models. Eventually we should be able to consider whether these models fit what we can observe.

Model 1: African + Roman = Roman dominance and end of African traits (assimilation)

This model proposes that following the Roman conquest Roman culture is introduced and dominates the previous African culture, which gradually dies out. In other words, the culture of the people of Africa was assimilated to Roman culture. In this model an African would in effect become a Roman and be so similar to a Roman that we might as well dispense with the term African and call everyone Roman. In this scenario we might imagine the importation of Roman political systems, religion, building types, city forms, art, language, social organization, etc. We should be able to see 'things Roman' appearing in Africa and 'things African' disappearing.

Model 2: African + Roman = African traits continue to dominate and Roman traits fail to become established (rejection)

This model is more or less the opposite of the first, and the political domination of Rome has little or no effect upon the African people and their culture. Here we might expect to find evidence for politico-military control but little or no evidence for Roman culture or the acceptance of a Roman identity. This is perhaps the model we might expect to encounter in frontier zones at the limits of the Roman empire. It might also prevail in a scenario where a traditional society chose to reinforce its own traditions by explicitly rejecting 'things Roman' and consciously promoting its own cultural identity as a counter to Roman influence.

Model 3: African + Roman = African persistence and no evidence of Roman traits dominating (separation)

This scenario sees African culture surviving following the Roman conquest, and where Roman culture is visible it does not replace pre-existing practice. Here we might imagine a *laissez-faire* attitude on the part of the Roman state, allowing the conquered people to carry on in their previous ways and the African people not needing to, or wanting to, adopt Roman customs, practices, forms of representation and cultural identity. In this model we might expect to find Roman and African traits remaining separate but co-existing (peacefully or otherwise) without significant alteration.

Model 4: African + Roman = Afro-Roman cultural mixing (fusion)

This model proposes that the combination of a Roman conquest and an African context led to the creation of a new and vital mixture, a cultural fusion of African and Roman traits. In this scenario we might expect to find cultural elements which may be originally Roman but are reworked in the African context to produce something new and different. Perhaps we need a new term for the result – something like Afro-Roman or Romano-African culture. In the previous exercise the temples of Saturn, Mercury and Caelestis were all marked as having both Roman and African characteristics, both in the deities worshipped and in the form of the temples, suggesting that there has been a mixing of cultures. This combining of deities is known as syncretism, and you have already encountered it in the essay 'Religion in the Roman world', which you read in Block Three.

We will now move on to consider a set of studies from Africa. Each will use different forms of evidence to demonstrate that our theoretical approach may be applied in a variety of circumstances. In each of these you should be thinking about which of the four models outlined above seems to fit the evidence best.

The building of Thugga

So far we have been considering aspects of Thugga without taking into account the chronology of the site and its monuments. The following table lists the public buildings and monuments of Thugga which are securely dated by inscriptions and gives the date (as near as possible) of construction along with an assessment of how African or Roman they are.

Date (AD)	Building	Roman?	African?	Reason
late Tiberius (14–37)	Temple of Caesar	✓	✗	Imperial cult
36–7	Forum and square in front of the temple to the emperor	✓	✗	Forum is typically Roman
36–7	Shrine of Saturn	✓	✓	Saturn is Roman and Punic god
36–7	Arch	✓	✗	Typically Roman monument
30s	Temple and statues	?	?	No details
30s	Temple of Ceres (square plus stone columns)	✓	✓	Ceres is Roman and Punic goddess
30s	Temple of Concordia	✓	✗	Concordia is Roman goddess
Caligula? (37–41)	Arch	✓	✗	Typically Roman monument
Claudius (41–54)	Small shrine of Jupiter	✓	✗	Jupiter is Roman god
48	Statue of Augustus	✓	✗	Augustus was Roman

Date (AD)	Building	Roman?	African?	Reason
54	Market	✓	✗	Typically Roman building
54	Small temple	?	?	No details
Hadrian (117–38)	Two temples of Concordia	✓	✗	Concordia is Roman goddess
Hadrian (117–38)	Temple of Fortuna	✓	✗	Fortuna is Roman goddess
Hadrian? (117–38)	Small apsidal temple to Augustan Piety	✓	✓	Augustan Piety is a Roman cult but temple is not Roman style
Antoninus Pius (138–61)	Portico round forum	✓	✗	Forum is typically Roman
Antoninus Pius (138–61)	Temple of Minerva	✓	✗	Minerva is Roman goddess
Marcus Aurelius (161–80)	Capitol	✓	✗	Capitol is typically Roman
Marcus Aurelius (161–80)	Theatre	✓	✗	Theatre is typically Roman
Marcus Aurelius (161–80)	Substantial temple	?	?	No details
Commodus (180–92)	Square and portico by forum	✓	✗	Forum is typically Roman
Commodus (180–92)	Temple of Mercury by capitol	✓	✓	Temple is African style and god is Roman
Commodus (180–92)	Shrine	?	?	No details
mid 180s	Aqueduct attached to southern baths	✓	✗	Aqueduct is typically Roman
Septimius Severus (193–211)	Large temple of Saturn	✓	✓	Temple is African style and god is Roman and African
Septimius Severus (193–211)	Arch to emperors	✓	✗	Typically Roman monument
Caracalla (211–17)	Temple	?	?	No details
Alexander Severus (222–35)	Circus or race-track	✓	✗	Typically Roman building

Date (AD)	Building	Roman?	African?	Reason
Alexander Severus (222–35)	Temple of Caelestis (semi-circular)	✓	✓	Temple is Roman and African style and goddess is African
Alexander Severus (222–35)	Triumphal arch to emperor for *libertas* or tax privileges	✓	✗	Typically Roman monument
Alexander Severus (222–35)	Temple	?	?	No details
Alexander Severus (222–35)	Temple of Fortuna	✓	✗	Fortuna is Roman goddess
Gallienus (261–8?)	Licinian baths	✓	✗	Baths are typically Roman and copy the ground plan of baths in Rome
mid third century	Temple of Tellus	✓	✓	Temple is African style and goddess is African and Roman
264	Portico	?	?	No details
Diocletian (284–305)	Temple of Genius Patriae	✓	✗	Cult is typically Roman
Diocletian (284–305)	Portico of temple of Mater Deum	✓	✗	Cult is typically Roman

Some of these buildings have survived and been excavated, while others have not. You have seen some of them in the video sequence 'Exploring Thugga'. The construction of these public and religious buildings is itself one aspect of the Romanization of the pre-Roman city of Thugga, and we must also remember that the practice of commemorating the dedication of a building with an inscription is itself a very Roman tradition. Therefore, we should perhaps expect this collection of evidence to favour more Roman aspects of the cultural milieu.

Plate 5.3 in the Illustrations Book illustrates when the main periods of building activity took place. The impression given by the graph is of a high degree of activity in the first half of the first century AD, which drops off rapidly and then rises to a second peak in the second half of the second century before gradually reducing again. This observed pattern roughly corresponds with the broader pattern of building dedications derived from North Africa as a whole (Jacques, 1989, pp.242–3), although the peak in the first half of the first century is more pronounced at Thugga. This suggests that the pattern at Thugga is not exceptional but part of a wider pattern of development common to Africa, although not necessarily other parts of the empire where similar evidence has been gathered (Duncan-Jones, 1990, pp.57–67).

An attractive possibility in interpreting this evidence is to see the pattern as a first wave of Romanizing building dedications in the early first century, establishing a Roman character for the city, and then later a second peak of building dedications as the city flourishes in the later second century along with the rest of Africa. Does this suggestion hold up? We can investigate further by considering two factors: the types of building dedicated and the identity and status of the person(s) who were the dedicants (see Plate 5.4) (Duncan-Jones, 1990, pp.178–82).

If we look first at the buildings from the first half of the first century, we see that most of them were temples. The earliest is a 'temple of Caesar'; we know no more, but it was probably a temple dedicated to Julius Caesar or Augustus: a more Roman and politically laden monument would be hard to imagine. The following three monuments – the forum and square in front of the temple to the emperor, a shrine of Saturn, and an arch – were all dedicated by one Postumius Chius. We have little to go on, but his name does not rule out the possibility that he was a Roman citizen or a freedman. The forum and arch at least are clearly in the Roman urban tradition; the former is of major importance to city life and represents the formal creation of a Roman-style town centre. The third building, the shrine of Saturn, is slightly more ambivalent because Saturn was both a Punic and a Roman deity (see p.28).

The next monument, a temple and statues, was restored by Licinius Tyrannus, who also built the temple of Ceres (a popular goddess introduced to Carthage in 396 BC), and his wife built the temple of Concordia (the goddess of Peace). Licinius Tyrannus was a freedman of Marcus Licinius Marcius, and the temple of Ceres was dedicated to the health of Marcus Licinius Rufus, his patron. The small shrine of Jupiter dedicated in the reign of Claudius bore an informative inscription. The shrine was built and jointly paid for by L. Iulius L.F. Crassus, a name suggesting that his family may have gained citizenship under Julius Caesar. Part of his career is listed, and he was military tribune in the Twenty-first Legion Rapacis, as well as a *duovir* and a *duovir quinquennalis* – the most senior civic position. He is also described as *patronus pagi*: that is, patron of the community of Roman citizens at Thugga. The shrine was also paid for by another citizen, C. Pomponius L.F. Restitutus. Thus we have a distinguished soldier and leader of the Roman community donating a shrine to the most important of Roman gods, Jupiter. So far all the donors seem to have been freedmen or Roman citizens, but in AD 48 one Iulius Venustus dedicated a statue of Augustus. Not an extraordinary act in itself, but we also know that Iulius Venustus was the son of one Thinoba, an office holder in the *civitas* of non-Roman citizens in Thugga. We do not know the hows and whys of this, but it clearly demonstrates a beginning of Africans performing typically Roman civic acts. It also demonstrates the adoption of a Roman form of name by Iulius Venustus, as opposed to the traditional African form of 'X son of Y', as on the Punic mausoleum. Despite these clearly Roman traits, we know from other inscriptions that the political organization of the *civitas* survived, and it was governed by officials with the Punic title of *suffete* rather than the Roman magistrate.

In AD 54 we again encounter M. Licinius Rufus – this time donating the market – and he is described as *patronus pagi* and also as a cavalry commander in Syria. In the reign of Hadrian (117–38) a pair of temples was dedicated to the deities Concordia and Frugifer and Liber Patus by the brothers M. and A. Gabinius. They are further described as sons of the manager of imperial estates around Thugga and also as *patronus pagi et civitatis*, meaning patrons of both the Roman citizen *pagus* and the 'indigenous' *civitas*. So by the second century we begin to see the same individuals playing a leading role in both the citizen and non-citizen communities. Later donations are by members of some of the families we have already encountered – the Licinii and the Gabini – but monuments are also dedicated by other families (particularly the Marcii) and individuals. The temple of Mercury by the capitol, which seems to have some elements of an African temple plan, was built in the reign of Commodus (180–92) by Q. Pacuvius Saturus and his wife Nahania Victoria, according to the will of their son M. Paccuvius Felix Victorianus (Figure 5.3). Here we have a couple, one with an apparently Roman name and the other with a clearly non-Roman *praenomen*. This suggests the possibility of a marriage between citizens of whom one (at least) has an African name. By AD 205 in the reign of Septimius Severus the city of Thugga had received the status of a *municipium liberum*, which would have ended the division between the *pagus* and the *civitas* and so united the people of the city and given them the same civic and legal rights.

Exercise

Which of the four models of cultural interaction do you think best fits the evidence you have encountered in Thugga? Write down your choice (or choices), and note down the evidence which supports your choice.

Discussion

You may have found that one or more of the models fitted the evidence, or that some parts of the evidence fitted one model but others fitted a different model. Don't be surprised by this because our models are just that – models. They are not full-blown explanations or exhaustive interpretations. They are intended to be aids to interpretation, to stimulate thought, open possibilities and debates. I am not going to provide a detailed discussion here of how the evidence from Thugga fits the models. There is, though, more discussion later in this section when the models are reviewed in the light of the further evidence you are now going to look at.

African Red Slip ware

Between about 30 BC and AD 75 the most common type of ceramic tableware in the empire was *terra sigillata* (often known as Samian ware). This was a shiny red-surfaced ceramic which was first made in Arezzo in Tuscany, Italy and then widely imitated in many areas such as Campania, Rome, southern and eastern Gaul, and Asia Minor. The forms of this pottery were typically cups, bowls, plates and dishes. Beyond the areas where it was produced, the pottery was widely traded and it has been found on countless sites, including North African sites from the Atlantic to the Nile. In many of the areas where the *terra sigillata* was imitated by local potters, the original Italian prototypes were closely copied and there was little or no innovation in the shapes or forms of decoration. However, in the region of Carthage workshops were established before the middle of the first century AD which produced pottery that initially copied the shapes of the Italian wares, even though its colour and texture were slightly different (see Plate 5.5). Later a range of new shapes and forms were developed that broke free from the Italian originals and began a tradition of tableware manufacture which continued until the latter part of the seventh century AD. No ancient name for this pottery has survived, but it is known to archaeologists as African Red Slip ware because of its distinctive bright orange glossy surface created by the application of a slip to the vessels. In the second century African Red Slip ware became the most common tableware in the Mediterranean area, and in most places replaced the Italian *terra sigillata* and its other imitators (see Plate 5.6). Although originally Italian in inspiration and function, the fine ware developed a range of original shapes and decoration, and new forms, particularly large shallow dishes, became common. How much this spread of African material culture was due to technological superiority, economic production, changes in eating practices or simply changes in fashion is still the subject of study.

Exercise

Consider which of our four models best fits the case of African Red Slip ware. Write down your choice (or choices), and note down the evidence which supports your choice.

Discussion

Although you only have limited evidence to go on, this case study is more clear cut than the previous ones. It is discussed further when the models are reassessed.

African mosaics: things Roman and things African?

Between the second and the fifth centuries a thriving tradition of mosaic floor decoration developed in North Africa (see Figure 5.4). There is only limited evidence for the dating of African mosaics, but the earliest seem to be closely influenced by Italian interior design, particularly stucco wall plaster, wall painting and monochrome mosaic floors. We can investigate this by looking at examples from the early second and third centuries. Look now at Colour Plates 5.1–5.4 and watch the two brief video sequences, 'Mosaic from Acholla' (t.c.23:20–25:43) and 'Mosaic from La Chebba' (t.c.25:48–28:03).

As you have just heard on the video, these kinds of compositions (see Figure 5.5 on p.26) are very similar to the details found in Italian interior decoration, for example in the buildings of Pompeii just before its destruction or in the *Domus Aurea*, the palace built by Nero in Rome (see Plate 5.7). So in this case the African mosaics seem to be reproducing motifs and styles of composition which were current in Italy at the time. Through the second and third centuries African mosaics developed their own repertoire of motifs and styles, and the prevalent types of mosaics diverged from their Italian counterparts. So, for example, the mosaic in Colour Plate 5.5, with its use of colour and vegetal motifs in a geometric pattern, displays a set of characteristics not found elsewhere.

The mosaic may be showing new decorative styles but the central panel, which sits awkwardly slightly off-centre in the mosaic, shows a very traditional Hellenistic figure of a poet or playwright reading a scroll in front of theatre masks. Alongside the popularity of geometric patterning, a major development in African mosaics was the use of figured compositions on a white background – see, for example, the mosaic of Neptune and the four seasons in Colour Plate 5.6.

A very popular theme in these mosaics is the illustration of hunting scenes, as for example the mosaic from El Djem in Colour Plate 5.7. Within its geometric border the mosaic may be divided into three sections forming a narrative of a hare hunt. At the top two horsemen

Figure 5.4 *Excavation of a mosaic floor, Chott Meriem near Sousse, Tunisia. DAI neg. no.55.1314. (Photo: Sichtermann/German Archaeological Institute, Rome)*

and a hunter with a spear are moving through a wood. In the middle the hounds and their handler are approaching a hare hiding in a bush. In the lower part of the scene the horsemen and hounds are pursuing the hare. The overall composition is very different to the earlier mosaics. The mosaic has a narrative of the progress of the hunt. There is a vitality and sense of movement which is lacking in the earlier mosaics: the

Figure 5.5 *Border with grotesque head from the 'Baths of Trajan', early second century* AD, *Acholla. Bardo Museum, Tunis. (Photo: P. Perkins)*

figures are not as meticulously moulded and less detail is seen in the drapery and plants, for example. The very schematic shadows are used to provide a ground level for the figures.

Another theme which became popular in African mosaics was the circus (see Plate 5.8). The circus had its origins in Rome at the Circus Maximus, but the popularity of the chariot races spread and in Africa they were particularly popular throughout the Roman period and even later into the Byzantine period (see Colour Plate 5.8).[1] Even small towns such as Thugga had a circus. Elsewhere in the empire only the largest towns and provincial capitals had a circus. The mosaic in Plate 5.8 (and seen in the 'Exploring Thugga' video, t.c.17:15–17:30) shows both the exterior and the interior of a circus. Three sides of the circus are shaded by an awning and empty rows of seats are shown on the fourth. Four chariots are shown, although there are eight starting gates on the right of the circus. The charioteer at the top right is carrying the palm of victory, as is the charioteer Eros from Thugga shown in the video

1 Please note that the caption to Colour Plate 5.8 is incorrect. It should read 'Chariot race in the circus from Gafsa, Tunisia, sixth century AD. Bardo Museum, Tunis. (Photo: Bardo Museum)'.

(t.c.17:30–17:49). In the mosaic from Gafsa (Colour Plate 5.8) emphasis is placed upon the spectators as well as the circus action.

Exercise

Consider which of our four models of cultural interaction best fits the evidence of the African mosaics sketched out here. Write down your choice (or choices), and note down the evidence which supports your choice.

Discussion

The mosaics display a variety of influences, and it is possible to identify Roman and Hellenistic traits. Uniquely African traits are harder to identify, but this style of mosaic with coloured figures on a white ground can clearly be seen as developing in Africa and neighbouring areas; it can be contrasted with different styles which were common in Asia Minor, Italy, Gaul or Britain. The mosaics are discussed further below.

Houses at Carthage, Bulla Regia and Thugga

Your next exercise is to watch again the video on houses of the Roman élite (video cassette 1, t.c.2:11:38–2:51:32). The video presents houses from different parts of the empire. Before you watch you may find it useful to review the notes you took in the exercises relating to the video in section 4.1 of Block Three.

Lisa Nevett has presented a wide-ranging investigation of houses in several parts of the empire and shown how they can provide evidence for expressions of culture and identity. Overall the video provides a broad context for the houses you have seen at Thugga and Bulla Regia. They can be seen as having connections with different aspects of the culture of the Roman empire. Some elements are shared, such as the use of the house as a location for display of status and access to Greek culture, or the use of courtyards and axial arrangements, or characteristic styles of decoration. From the evidence presented in the video we can consider the houses in a number of ways. Are the building materials and their decoration the same in all parts of the empire? Is the arrangement of rooms and their sizes and relationships to one another similar in these different places? Did similar parts of the houses have similar functions? Are there the possibilities for the same social interpretations of the houses in different areas? Can we contrast a 'Roman' house with an 'African' house, or for that matter a Greek house? We can ask how much they are African or Roman or Afro-Roman.

Exercise

Consider which of our four models of cultural interaction best fits the evidence from studying the houses in Africa and elsewhere. Write down your choice (or choices), and note down the evidence which supports your choice.

Discussion

It's easy enough to see which houses we might call African – either those similar to the Punic houses in Carthage or the later houses in Africa, allowing the geographical location to be the defining factor (see Figure 5.6). However, what about the houses that might be 'Roman'? Do we take the houses in Pompeii as typically Roman? And if so, where does that leave the houses in Ephesus? The question is complex because the houses share some features but in other ways they are distinct from one another. We also need to remember that there are chronological differences to consider. The Punic houses were abandoned following the Roman conquest; all the houses in Pompeii were destroyed in AD 79; and the rest of those in Africa date from the second century onwards, with later alterations and reorganizations. It is also important to consider whether the houses are comparable as the homes of élite members of society in different parts of the empire, or whether each is the home of a different class or kind of person. There is more discussion below.

Reconsideration of the models and their suitability

Now that we have studied a variety of sources of evidence from Africa, it is possible to reconsider how well our four models of cultural interaction fit the evidence.

The building of Thugga

In summary, most of the buildings we have dedications for in Thugga are of a Roman type. The exceptions are temples to gods or goddesses who were also worshipped in pre-Roman Africa or at least had strict equivalents, such as Baal and Saturn and Juno and Caelestis. This evidence would seem to suggest that this African city was very receptive of Roman models for building types, therefore fitting best into model 1. Nevertheless the adoption of Roman-style buildings seems to have been gradual, and with the exception of the forum the main Roman-style buildings – the capitol, theatre, baths and circus – were not built until the later second century and the third century. So it would seem that if

Figure 5.6 *Punic house on Byrsa hill, early second century BC, Carthage. (Photo: P. Perkins)*

model 1 fits best, it was a gradual transition rather than an abrupt change.

However, we must remember that we know extremely little about the urban form and building of the pre-Roman city of Thugga. There does seem to have been some survival of the earlier urban form of the city, since to the north-west the city remained largely confined within the Punic city walls and the street plan of the centre of the city may also be a Punic survival. There is also excavated evidence to suggest that a temple to Baal preceded the Severan temple of Saturn. This would seem to suggest that there was some survival of pre-Roman urban forms and buildings, which would fit best with model 2 or 3 suggesting either rejection of Roman forms such as regular grids of streets or co-existence of Roman and pre-Roman urban structures.

The identification of two sectors in the people of Thugga, the Roman *pagus* and the African *civitas*, fits well with the third model – separation of indigenous and Roman peoples. However, through time this division disappears as the town grows in status and becomes first a *municipium* by AD 205 and then a *colonia*, suggesting that model 4 – fusion – might be more appropriate. This gradual merging of the communities in the city and their governments runs in parallel with a shifting identity of the donors of the buildings. It is just about possible to discern a shift from Roman donors to a combination of donors where some are Roman and some individuals have African names or descent. This too best fits model 4 – fusion as the result of cultural interaction. Fusion can also be seen in the developed city of Thugga, which by the time it became a *colonia* combined both African, Roman and Greek cultural influences.

This discussion illustrates the fact that no one model has the power to explain all of our observations. Different models may fit different parts of the evidence, and different models might fit the evidence at different periods of the progress of cultural interaction, so dominance may be followed by separatism and then fusion. This observation underlines the fact that cultural interaction is an ongoing dynamic process.

African Red Slip ware

The African Red Slip ware provides a clear case of an Italian range of artefacts being first imported to Africa and used, but then being copied and produced in Africa. The African production then develops its own characteristics and identity as an African product. This fits model 4 best, where the Italian prototype is taken over to produce something new, original and Afro-Roman.

Mosaics

The question of the mosaics can be considered at various levels. As a flooring technique its origin lies in the Hellenistic east, but in the Punic world plaster floors inset with small squared stones, sometimes in geometric patterns, are also known, as you have seen in the video of the houses at Carthage. So it's not possible simply to see mosaic floors as a part of Roman culture which came to be dominant in Africa, because mosaics themselves are not a purely Roman tradition. Nevertheless, it is not possible to see them just as an African phenomonen either, because what is represented on the mosaics often has a recognizable Roman component. The earlier mosaics from Acholla have compositional and stylistic similarities to painting and stucco in central Italy. Likewise many of the themes in figured mosaics can be related to Graeco-Roman mythology or Roman cultural practices such as the circus or amphitheatre (see Figure 5.7 overleaf).

Taken as a whole the mosaics from Africa can be seen as distinct from those elsewhere, and together form a group which can be distinguished from mosaics common elsewhere. This suggests model 4, cultural fusion, is perhaps most appropriate.

Houses

In the case of the houses it is more difficult to differentiate clearly between 'Roman' and 'African' if we accept that the atrium–peristyle house is not the only form of dwelling we can identify as typically Roman. Nevertheless, it seems that the houses in Africa do represent a fusion of elements – African, Roman and Hellenistic – suggesting that model 4 might be most appropriate in the case of the houses at Bulla Regia. They combine a Roman symmetry with a Hellenistic peristyle and an African sunken court decorated with mosaics. Overall it seems very much as if we are studying a fusion of cultural elements which came together to create a vibrant culture. Furthermore, the houses seem to function in a similar social way as a setting for the display of wealth, education and status.

There are other areas of cultural interaction which we have not considered, and various of the models may be appropriate in different cases. So, for example, Latin became the official language of administration and commemoration on stone, suggesting that model 1 would fit best, whereas sporadic rebellions indicate that some aspects of Roman culture were actively rejected, suggesting model 2 might be more appropriate in some areas. The evidence we have just considered can be interpreted with reference to our four models of cultural interaction, but it should be clear that in individual cases and all the cases together the models do not fit exactly nor do they fully explain the evidence. What is more they are not necessarily mutually exclusive: that is to say, more than one of them may be seen to apply to the same evidence, either at the same time or following from each other. This is due partly to the simplicity of the models but also to the fact that the original premise – that there is something we can identify as African and something we can identify as Roman which we can compare and contrast

Figure 5.7   *Mosaic and marble floor from a large town house, third century* AD, *Carthage.* *(Photo: P. Perkins)*

– was itself a polarization of the issues. At this stage of the course you have studied enough of the Roman world to know that it was very diverse and contained a broad range of experiences. Just as the concept of 'Roman' is multi-faceted and variable, so is the concept of 'African'. When the two come together it is perhaps not surprising that the resulting cultural mix is rich and complex.

So far in our investigation of cultural interaction between Africa and Rome we have been dealing largely with archaeological evidence, and our interpretative perspective has been very much one of 'us' looking back at 'them' – the Romans or Africans. For the next part of the block we will change that viewpoint and, using literary sources, consider how the Romans looked at the Africans and see how that may, in turn, inform our point of view. In doing this we need to construct a different kind of checklist to distinguish between Roman and African identities. African leaders presented in the pages of Roman authors can be depicted in a variety of ways: as possessing ethnic qualities alien and threatening to the Roman ideal, as Romanized and admirable, as Romanized but picking up bad habits from Rome. The important point is that all these presentations of 'Africanness' (*Africanitas*) are penned by men steeped in *Roman* cultural traditions. *Romanitas* is their constant benchmark.

Part Two: Literary characterization of Africa and Africans

BY PAULA JAMES

2.1 Figures in a landscape: Roman authors and North Africa

In this part you will be reading a selection of prose and poetry spanning the late republican period to the end of the first century AD. Sallust and Livy were prose historians. Livy has already appeared in Block Two, and you have also encountered Virgil in Blocks One and Two. Lucan and Silius Italicus both carried on the Virgilian epic tradition, and they too will feature in the discussion about the 'literary' North Africa. The authors have been chosen for their vivid characterizations of 'barbarian' (non-Roman) leaders who opposed the empire or in some way stood in the way of its progress and expansion.

This part should help you to focus on the values *Roman* writers assigned to cultural traits. The traits themselves are a Roman construction. Even in those places where accounts of African actions might be accurate or at least verifiable by some physical evidence, the motives ascribed to the barbarians are grounded upon convenient and traditional assumptions about African characteristics. These characteristics 'explained' the enemy behaviour as far as the Roman historian was concerned. This makes for colourful reporting and on occasion produces such a plausible scenario that it is difficult to divorce literary 'facts' from historical ones. As you extend your understanding of the role of Roman literature, both romanticized legend and historical narrative, you will be simultaneously refining the concept of cultural stereotypes, including the stereotypical ideal Romans had constructed for their own identity. Essay Ten, which you will be asked to read at the end of section 2.3, discusses many of these issues. You should continue the good practice you have developed in your study of Blocks One to Four. This means taking into account the personal and social circumstances of the authors you encounter, being aware of the genres in which they have chosen to work, and reminding yourself about ideological agendas they have inherited and adapted.

It is important that you continue to exercise your critical faculties by taking full advantage of the familiar exercise and discussion format. At this stage in the course you may feel encouraged and confident enough to identify issues of your own as you read through the extracts provided. I shall be reminding you of the conventions and traditions of literary genres which are so important to our use of literature as evidence. Although Block One probably seems a long way back in the course, in your study of literary extracts in Blocks Two to Four you have been steadily building upon the skills of contextualization and interpretation you first encountered in the portrayal of Actium by the Augustan poets. As with the poetry, the literary and political agendas of the authors on North Africa have to be taken into account, and how they might be putting a personal stamp upon the traditions and conventions of their chosen medium.

Carthaginian Dido and the shape of things to come: Virgil's *Aeneid* 1 and 4

You have met the epic poem, the *Aeneid*, before so you may wish to remind yourself of the story and of Virgil's poetic and political standpoint during the principate of Augustus (see Block One, section 1.1). Virgil played an important part in contributing to the portrayal of Augustus as a guarantor of the glorious destiny of Rome. The war with Antony and Cleopatra rapidly became a cautionary tale (and naturally Octavian encouraged his poetic circle to help this along) in which Antony's seduction into alien ways and foreign loyalties illustrated dangers other than military attacks for Romans and their empire. The story of Dido, who became passionately embroiled with Aeneas and died tragically by her own hand when her lover continued his search for the promised land, is a famous episode in the epic.

However, Aeneas' involvement with Dido and the delay in his mission (he takes up residence in Carthage and begins to supervise the building of the city) invited comparisons, even in the ancient commentators on Virgil, with the humiliating situation of Antony, a Roman captivated by a foreign queen. If Aeneas is viewed a potential prototype for Antony as well as a good role model for Augustus, then Dido becomes as dangerous and hostile to the Roman dream as Cleopatra was to be for the reality of Roman power.

I shall be asking you to look at a selection from Book 1 of the *Aeneid*, the arrival of the Trojans on an unknown shore, shipwrecked by the vindictiveness of the goddess Juno, and Book 4, their departure with the curses of Dido ringing in the ears of the readers. What I am hoping to do here is to tease out the Roman agenda as far as African enemies were concerned: these heroes and villains of history might be as much admired as hated, but one persistent pattern emerges which I find useful as a reference point. The African temperament as reconstructed by Roman writers was consistently volatile, their nature passionate and their friendship likely to turn to bitter enmity in a short space of time with acts of unprovoked aggression. Punic faithlessness is a constant refrain in historians such as Livy.

In the eyes of historical and poetic commentators of the time, an uncertainty principle operated wherever Romans engaged in business or war on African territory. I shall be asking you to explore the first passage for hints of menace and volatility in the situation the Trojans find themselves in. At the beginning of the first book, the Trojan company has been blown off course to the coast of North Africa and has to negotiate a potentially hostile shore. However, things turn out much better than expected. Not only has Aeneas' fleet survived the terrible storm intact, but also Venus, his goddess mother, is there to assist them. Disguised as a huntress, she fills in the background of the place and the courage and enterprise of the Sidonian queen in acquiring a settlement for herself and her followers on North African soil.

Exercise

Read extract 5.1a in the Supplementary Texts (from Book 1 of the *Aeneid*), and note the precautions taken by Venus to ensure her son a good reception in Carthage. What threatening undercurrents can you detect here?

Discussion

One interesting aspect of Virgil's portrayal of Carthage and Carthaginian Dido is the likelihood of a mixed reception for the Trojans. In spite of Dido's protestations, assurances and actions, Venus does not trust the Tyrians. Venus suspects that the goddess Juno is behind this warm welcome and that it could well be a trap. This is clearly stated in the passage. Well done if you picked up also on Aeneas' concern about his son, who is quickly summoned to the banquet (is there fear of an ambush here?). Ascanius is instructed to bring gifts, many of which have a tragic resonance – 'salvaged/ From Troy's ruins' – including a possibly ominous veil of 'Argive Helen'.

Without access to the original Latin you couldn't know this, but there is a telling moment where the English word 'equivocation' is used by the translator for the Latin *bilingues*, literally double-tongued. The phrase *domum timet ambiguam*, which can be translated literally as 'she fears the two-faced house', is covered by the statement that 'Venus felt uneasy about her [Dido's] hospitality'.

It is possible to produce an even richer reading of this passage. On the surface, the Trojans and Tyrians are united by similar experiences, by a distant kinship and, to a certain extent, a common culture. For instance, Aeneas is able to fulfil expectations of *xenia* (reciprocal hospitality) on his side by producing expensive gifts for

Dido and her court. Virgil presents us with a 'genre' scene, a set piece with certain formulae and a particular style of description, but he has overlaid it with Roman concerns about the 'historic' enemy the Carthaginians were destined to become. In their commentary on Book 1, H.E. Gould and J.L. Whiteley point out that 'Vergil writing of the foundation of Carthage in about 800 B.C. assigns to Dido and her people the reputation which the Romans attributed to the historic Carthaginians of five centuries later' (1947, p.122).

As ever with a literary text of this type, it is wise to look for other factors affecting Virgil's interpretation of Aeneas' legendary stopover in Carthage. I am quite convinced that he intentionally colours the characterization of Dido and her Tyrians with the 'hindsight' suggested by Gould and Whiteley. However, he is also following a Homeric and Hellenistic tradition in the scene you have just read. Homer's Odysseus and Apollonius' Jason (the epic *Argonautica*, written in the third century BC) both have to negotiate awkward and threatening situations in strange kingdoms. A goddess or god is dispatched to ensure a hospitable welcome. I have already raised the issue of hospitality; *xenia* (a custom sanctioned by Jupiter himself) was a delicate business for the giver and recipient. A complicating factor in the case of Aeneas and his people is the enmity of Juno. She is the patron goddess of the newly emergent Carthaginian city, so Venus is nervously awaiting some reprisal from her sister deity and takes extra precautions with the substitute of Cupid for Aeneas' son Ascanius. Giving Dido a grand passion for the Trojan prince will ensure his safety in her palace.

The fate of Dido reinforces an important theme of the *Aeneid*, that the destiny of Rome was to rule and that the establishment of its civilization in Italy could not be diverted, whatever the personal or even political cost. Carthaginian Dido, herself a refugee from Sidon, the original capital of Phoenicia, benefits from a sympathetic treatment by the poet. The queen and her people have established themselves in a fairly unforgiving terrain. Dido might have been wise to marry a local chieftain to ensure acceptance and support by the local nobility. In fact, her passion for Aeneas incites Iarbas, an indigenous royal and rejected suitor, to complain to the god Jupiter/Ammon about her bad taste and double standards.[2]

2 As you will see in the notes to the next extract, Iarbas is the son of Ammon (also known as Baal Hammon), an African god identified with the Roman god Jupiter.

Exercise

Read extract 5.1b (from Book 4) in the Supplementary Texts now. Think back to discussions about cultural mixing, especially in regard to religion and the gods, and the tendency to syncretize Roman and indigenous deities (Essay Nine, which you read in Block Three). What literary motives might Virgil have for introducing Iarbas at this point?

Discussion

I find this a very interesting interlude in Book 4. Iarbus is the result of a mixed 'marriage' (actually his African nymph mother was raped by Jupiter/Ammon). The local king is a combination of divine and mortal, African and Greek. The introduction of Iarbas serves as more than a convenient narrative device for alerting Jupiter to the state of affairs (no pun intended) in Carthage so that he actively intervenes and sends Aeneas on his way to Italy. (But if this is the primary literary motive you found – that is, to resolve the impasse the hero is in – it is a perfectly legitimate one.) There are some significant cultural assumptions in this passage. In some ways Iarbas' devotion to his father and his zealous worship connect him culturally with Roman reverence towards the greatest god. Iarbas' contempt for the effeminate Phrygians (the quip about their bonnets!) demonstrates this fictional African's aptitude for cultural stereotyping when it comes to foreigners from the east, and this characterization of them might have struck chords for a Roman readership. (Ironically, the Trojans would have shared the Asia Minor coast with Dido's people, the Phoenicians.)

On the other hand, it is rather shocking to hear Aeneas, father-to-be of the Roman race, degraded in this description. However, at this point in the story he is acting more as a decadent oriental prince than a heroic commander with responsibilities – hence Jupiter's speedy dispatch of Mercury to remind Aeneas of his mission. Iarbas' prayers are only partially answered with the rapid departure of his rival, because Dido commits suicide rather than turn to the scorned and smarting suitor who is waiting in the wings. Marrying an African king is not an option, as far as Dido is concerned: 'What shall I do? Shall I, who've been jilted, return to my former suitors? Go down on my knees for marriage to one of the Nomads, although time and again I have rejected their offers?' (*Aeneid* 4.534–6). In this case C. Day Lewis's translation does not quite do justice to the contempt Dido continues to feel for her indigenous neighbours. The Latin word *Nomas* is derogatory, referring to a restless Romany-style existence (although paradoxically it is the Trojan Aeneas who is on the move and who has proved unreliable), and the word for rejecting, *dedignor*, indicates strong disdain, not a polite refusal. Iarbas himself comes across as passionate to a fault. The failure to win Dido has severely rankled with him. All his actions, including the hundred altars awash with the blood of sacrifices, have demonstrated a proper respect for his divine father. He is unrestrainedly angry that this devotion has so far not been reciprocated. I shall return to this feature of African hot-headedness later.

Exercise

Now read the extract taken from the end of Book 4, the curse of Dido upon the descendants of Aeneas (6.1c). How sympathetic do you find the picture of the distraught queen? In the light of the actual welcome the Trojans were actually given in Book 1, what do you make of Dido's alternative scenario in the lines beginning, 'Why could I have not seized him?'

Discussion

Dido has clearly deteriorated from the dignified and majestic figure of goddess-like stature and beauty who was introduced to the reader in Book 1. It is interesting that many of her fine qualities are akin to Roman ideals for both a leader and a woman. In Book 4 she is praised for her loyalty to her murdered husband Sychaeus, making her like those virtuous Roman matrons who refused to remarry and were dubbed *univira* (meaning a woman who remained faithful for life to one man). Her care for her people and her steadfastness of purpose in the building of the city are scuppered along with her vows of fidelity to Sychaeus by the passion she conceives for Aeneas (and this destructive desire has been intensified, if not initiated, by the work of Cupid). However, I would say that Virgil begins at this point in the narrative to detach the Roman reader from the tragedy. This transformed Dido is already relishing the revenge to come through the scourge of Rome and Italy, Hannibal.

Dido has begun her speech on the theme of Aeneas' ingratitude and deception and her own gullibility in believing in his honour and dutifulness to family and country. The household gods are presented as tools of seduction, a cynical ploy to win trust and friendship. In an earlier plea to Aeneas not to leave Carthage, Dido's intermediary, her sister Anna, has been instructed to point out that the queen was undeserving of such a cruel desertion. She had not attacked or ill-treated the Trojan or his followers or desecrated the memory of Aeneas' dead father. Dido now dwells on the option of slaughter she could have chosen when the exiles were in her power. Dido's vengeful fancies with their tragic colouring – the serving of his son to Aeneas at a banquet (probably a reference to the legend of Procne and Tereus, in which a vengeful Procne served up their son as a meal for her husband) and the scattering of Aeneas himself over the sea (an allusion to Medea's murder of her brother Absyrtus) – also reveal something of Punic savagery towards their enemies.

I would suggest that the course of action that Dido describes as open to her when Aeneas arrived demonstrates the danger Carthage represented to this early wandering nation. Given the subsequent conflict between Carthage and Rome, the 'honeymoon' period between the first ruler of Carthage and the distant father of the Roman people was most definitely an aberration.

2.2   Prose pictures

The two historians Sallust and Livy were powerful and distinctive writers who covered the early conflicts of the republican period. Gaius Sallustius Crispus' *floruit*[3] was in the late republican period, but he is included for his influential 'shaping' of a famous African personality, Jugurtha. Sallust was Sabine in origin, born in territory about fifty-five miles north-east of Rome. He was very much embroiled in Roman politics and suffered expulsion from the senate in 50 BC under the censorship of Appius Claudius Pulcher. Sallust wrote a famous account of the conspiracy of Catiline, a disaffected son of Rome, against the government of Rome. His history of the foreign war against Jugurtha was at least partly inspired by its significance to Roman political life. He claimed to be drawing not just on existing histories and the memoirs of Roman commanders like Sulla, who had been 'at the front', but also on Punic sources translated for his benefit (*Jugurtha* 17.7). He was familiar with Africa since he fought there during the civil wars in the army of Julius Caesar and became the first governor of the new province of Numidia in 46 BC.

Sallust was not unusual in his approach and in having an ideological axe to grind. History for the practitioners of the discipline in the ancient world was invariably presented as an investigation into the events and figures of the past, but factual reconstruction was tempered and affected by an abiding concern with the author's contemporary world. Look back to the Livy extract from the Preface to Books 1–5 of the *Histories* (extract 2.4). It could be argued that the search for causes, patterns and trends

---

3 Latin for 'the time of their main literary output' (abbreviated as fl.).

which might explain the present is still very much the business of history. Sallust was certainly closer to the events he was reconstructing than a writer like Livy, who worked with a mixture of legend and the oral and anecdotal evidence of earlier times.

Both historians, however, had plenty of room for creative interpretation, as wars in the provinces were significantly distant from the historian's Roman audience, and even those who might have conflicting experiences, so far as particulars were concerned, could be reconciled to the general picture painted by a Sallust or a Livy. Dramatic reconstructions, the role of the individual in history, collective psychologies, regenerative and degenerative processes among peoples and societies at war: all these issues might be raised in the course of an (on the surface) factual chronology and resolved within an ethical and philosophical framework common to the educated élite.

Sallust contrasted the virtues of the old nobility, as attested in the commemorations of their funerals, with the vices and moral corruption of leading sections of society once the empire had expanded. The ease with which the Numidian king Jugurtha bribed his way out of Roman reprisals was a sure testament to the decadence that came with prosperity and a lack of foreign enemies. Your reading of the extracts from *The War with Jugurtha* will be in the nature of scene setting rather than passages for close interpretation. Sallust brings Jugurtha vividly alive and is admiring of his efforts to be a 'model' Roman. In the character sketch by Sallust, Jugurtha is seen as learning other, less sterling qualities and strategies from his Roman masters, which he then turned against them. Whatever indigenous 'type' emerges from the pages of Roman authors, the process is likely to reveal aspects of Roman identity more reliably than a model of genuine African ethnicity.

Exercise

Please read sections 6 to 8 followed by section 35 in the Sallust selection (extract 5.2). Note that in the intervening pages the account describes Jugurtha's encroachment upon other territory; he blatantly ignores the advice of Scipio in his dealings with the city and people of Rome. What, in Sallust's opinion, are Jugurtha's good qualities? How does he depict Jugurtha's manipulation of weaknesses in the Roman character?

Discussion

Jugurtha is introduced as a young man with enormous potential, and he is praised for combining a number of Roman virtues. He came, through an illegitimate line, from the dynasty of Masinissa, a family traditionally allied with Rome from the time of Hannibal. In the past, Rome had connived at Masinissa's expansion into the territory of Carthage once the Roman victory in North Africa was complete. From what you were told earlier about Sallust, you may have worked out for yourself that Roman venality and corruption are being deliberately brought into sharp relief by the utterances and actions of Jugurtha. The African leader managed to succeed over a number of years with his strategy of financial seduction, so much so that a large number of senators were eventually prosecuted for succumbing to his bribery.

Not even the massacre of the Italians at Cirta which prompted Rome to declare war on Jugurtha prevented his successful policy of buying off members of the ruling body by a judicious use of the client gift-giving system. Jugurtha's knowledge of the Roman way of things, the very Romanization of his character which Sallust's Scipio had noted, was turned against the interests of the empire in North Africa. Jugurtha was eventually defeated, captured and executed, but in Sallust's eyes his career had exposed the vulnerability of Roman morals in what this historian regarded as a time of decline and degeneration.

Let us now turn to Livy, roughly contemporary with Virgil and also writing during the relatively settled times of the first emperor, but still affectionately teased by Augustus for lingering republican sympathies. If you read the brief allusion to Livy in Wells, page 76, you will see that this Augustan historian was as convinced of the Roman right and fitness to rule as Virgil appears to be in his epic poetry. Goodman, pages 135–6, also emphasizes that Livy was recording the monumental 'labour' of Rome to achieve hegemony over Italy and the Mediterranean world. I am not suggesting that Livy wrote prose epic as such, but both he and Virgil would have shared a concept of Roman destiny, a sense of cumulative struggle towards empire divinely sanctioned and historically inevitable. The historian would not have questioned the pivotal position of Rome in the known world and the ultimate pointlessness of confrontation with it, whatever the nature of Roman government, aristocratic or autocratic.

Exercise

Please turn to Livy's description of the episode with Masinissa (extract 5.3). This episode in Africa's conflict with Rome pre-dates the period covered by Sallust. There are three elements to this episode which I would like you to concentrate upon: first, the spectacle of Syphax, the captured king; secondly, the portrayal of his rival Masinissa; and, thirdly, Scipio's attitudes towards these allegedly capricious North African allies.

It would also be useful to keep in mind the fact that passion for a woman perverts the alliance of both Syphax and Masinissa with Rome, and to note Livy's strong imagery to emphasize the dangerous situation her presence and persuasiveness had created.

Discussion

The downfall of Syphax – and Livy is honest enough about the tendency to exaggerate his greatness and position – has a very tragic ring to it. Syphax's fatal mistake was his passion for Sophonisba. Love had blinded him to the political promises he had made, and he had broken a sacred trust with the Romans. Scipio, the Roman commander, is disappointed and saddened at Syphax's behaviour. Syphax is reported as saying that his ruin began when he received a woman of Carthage into his household. Given the historic hostility between Carthage and Rome since the time of Dido, the themes of the episode Livy has constructed are beginning to take on a familiar hue. Syphax simply was not strong enough to withstand temptation. Nor is the danger over, since Masinissa, the new Numidian ally, is now in the same susceptible situation.

Masinissa also succumbs to the beauty and blandishments of Sophonisba. Although Livy presents the situation as a highly charged one emotionally and invests Sophonisba with rhetorical skills, persuasive in her pleas as well as almost irresistible in her attractions, on the other side he depicts the smitten Masinissa as characteristically (for his ethnicity) inflammable. The Roman commander, Scipio, has never fallen for a female captive, and his speech to Masinissa strongly suggests that Masinissa has potentially estranged himself from his Roman masters not just by an act of disloyalty but by displaying an un-Roman lack of self-control.

Going back to his ethnic roots was not a cause for celebration, and Masinissa is suitably chastened by Scipio's reproach. In fact, he is reduced to tears and in sufficient emotional turmoil to commit another impulsive act which Scipio had not anticipated or desired: that is, the sending of poison to Sophonisba. Thus the 'young and hot-blooded' Numidian 'imported an unnecessary note of tragedy' into the whole affair; we have shades of Dido here in the fate of Sophonisba.

The consolation to Masinissa, to distract him from the grief and bereavement, is an array of gifts, exotic but also laden with status of a specifically Roman type. This singles out Masinissa as worthy of a triumph and so functions as a high compliment as well as a 'comforter' for the distressed king. Ostentatious presents are very appealing. In Sallust the descendant of Masinissa, Jugurtha, is depicted as sophisticated and manipulative in a very similar style to Scipio and his methods. Livy is much more celebratory of Roman tactics and tacticians, and tends too to be totally sold upon the concept of volatility amongst elements of the African nation. It is possible to see Roman constructions of African identities diversifying in so far as Carthage is seen as the centre of subversion. Tribal leaders farther afield are sometimes gullible and manipulated. The Roman concept of a typical Numidian includes vulnerability to deep-seated passions, leading to breaches of war etiquette and unpredictable actions all around. The Carthaginians do not play by the Roman rules for more calculating reasons.

Livy's depiction of the Carthaginian Sophonisba brings in another dimension. He implies that her race, descended from the Phoenicians, is full of guile and invariably hostile to the ambitions of Rome. Throughout the wars with Carthage and the bitter struggle with Hannibal, Livy subscribes to the idea of Punic faithlessness. As I indicated earlier, this was a leitmotif of Roman rhetoric whenever they wished to justify the initiation of wars on Carthaginian territory. There was always a good reason to be discovered for acts of aggression which could be readily transformed into the discourse of defence.

Historical epic

Livy was not alone in depicting this tragic/romantic triangle of Sophonisba, Massinissa and Syphax. The longest Latin poem, consisting of 12,000 verses, took the Carthaginian wars as its epic historic subject-matter. This work, *Punica*, was the product of a long retirement. The author, Silius Italicus, survived through the rule of Tiberius, Gaius Caligula, Claudius, Nero, Vespasian, Titus, Domitian and Nerva. He lived long enough to see Trajan succeed Nerva. Silius had held political office; he was consul during the chaotic 'year of four emperors' when Nero had been overthrown and forced to suicide. He had also governed the province of Asia. His literary hero was Virgil (he restored Virgil's tomb at Naples and celebrated his birthday with great ceremony). Silius treated Virgil as his source for the early history of Carthage, and he extended the story of Dido and the Phoenician royal family in his epic, tracing the persecution of Dido's sister Anna by Iarbas and her subsequent flight to Italy.

Even contemporary commentators (and friends of Silius, the Younger Pliny for instance) felt that the epic *Punica* was more worthy than inspiring, but there are points of interest for us in our study of Roman ideas about African identities. Perhaps it is not surprising that Hannibal emerges as the hero, however hard Silius tries to keep the position for Scipio. Silius' Syphax fulfils his tragic promise in this poetic version of events, but there are distinct similarities with Livy, and Silius is very probably drawing on the historian's colourful elaboration for his epic material. Read the extract in your Supplementary Texts (5.4). Do note the emphasis on having a god in common and the rites Scipio and Syphax perform to cement the Roman/Numidian alliance. As with Aeneas' reception at the court of Dido, there is an ominous subtext to the hopeful beginning.

2.3 Lucan and the unforgiving landscape of Libya

We stay in the time zone of the first century AD but move to the reign of Nero and the poetry of Lucan, one of several artistic casualties once the emperor held power in his own right. Lucan was a nephew of Seneca and suffered a similar fate (forced to commit suicide by Nero) when he was implicated in a conspiracy against the emperor, but he had also incited the jealousy of Nero because of his talents as a poet. Lucan's epic on the civil wars between Pompey and Caesar is a powerful but lugubrious work, very much of its time, a period which has been described as 'a world poised on the brink of spiritual bankruptcy' (Ahl, 1976, p.17).

For key figures (associated with the Stoical school of philosophy) of the so-called Silver Age of Latin literature, this was a sorry state of affairs – the contemporary decadence of a society which no longer had serious rivals for power and therefore had turned in upon itself; in moral and ethical terms it had begun to self-destruct. Lucan traced the rot back beyond the principate to the first Caesar, Julius that is, and the effective end of the republic and *libertas*. For the nineteenth-century poet Shelley, Lucan was the great voice of protest against tyranny and oppression (Ahl, 1976, p.58). Later in the nineteenth century Lucan's negative view of the energized and conquering hero Caesar ensured him a bad press among nations with imperialist ambitions, and until relatively recently the twentieth century relegated him to 'the graveyard of literary history' (Ahl, 1976, p.61).

I hope that you will find Lucan's approach to the epic genre an interesting contrast with Virgil's. Like the historians you encountered earlier, Lucan looks to the past to make a judgement on the present. Unlike Virgil, he did not live in the days of hope, as a succession of emperors had demonstrated the degenerative process at work at the highest level of administration and government. Therefore he perceived and powerfully portrayed early cracks in the fabric of the empire. His choice of the civil wars as the subject-matter for a tragic poetic narrative was apposite because the key battleground of Pompey and Caesar – the province of Africa – emerged with the following symbolic dimension.

Silius Italicus in his epic *Punica*, which deals with the Carthaginian Wars, actually wished Carthage was still standing because without it Rome had reached a nadir in the quality of its leadership and lifestyles: 'Yet no sooner was Carthage destroyed than Rome fell prey, not to a foreign enemy but to herself' (Ahl, 1976, p.82). The Carthage connection was an obvious one to make since the final clash of the civil wars took place at Thapsus, 'not far from Zama where Scipio Africanus had defeated Hannibal, and the conflict occurred exactly a century after the final destruction of Carthage' (Ahl, 1976, p.82).

Ahl points out that the paradoxes pile up: both opposing armies were commanded by descendants of the Scipio family. Links with the *gens*[4] of Metellus made one of the leaders, in addition, a relative of the conqueror of Jugurtha. Cato (on the Pompeian side) brought with him the famous legacy of a previous Cato, the stern martinet who had urged the destruction of Carthage (*delenda est Carthago*) at every senate meeting after the defeat of Hannibal. Lucan was not the first to parade Thapsus, the scene of internecine strife, as the vengeance not only of Hannibal but also of Jugurtha, very definitely a Roman 'own goal' in the game of destiny (see Horace, *Odes* 2.1, 25–8).

Exercise

I would like you now to turn to the passages from Lucan's *The Civil War* in your Supplementary Texts (extract 5.5), and to make your own judgement of the effectiveness of this extremely bizarre and bloodthirsty scene. Use the questions below as a guide to your interpretation of the extract:

1   What kind of mix of myth and history do you detect here?

2   How does Cato emerge from this trial of courage and endurance?

3   Why do you think Lucan brought the Libyan desert alive in this graphic and barely credible way?

Discussion

1   There is no divine machinery in Lucan's historical epic. He gives the mythical explanation for the surfeit of serpents in the desert to a superstitious peasant, and confesses his own failure to come

---

4 A race, clan, family group; numbers of families linked together by a common name and common religious cults or rites, usually claiming a common ancestor. The Metelli were a notable aristocratic family who had a history of campaigning in Africa.

up with an alternative explanation. Lucan relishes all the ramifications of the Medusa legend that he has available to him. The prolonged episode seems designed to shake the Stoical resolve of Cato, who has refused to probe into the future fate of himself and his men or into the long-term outcome of the war. The Medusa story certainly adds colour, and removes us from the theatre of war and into the realms of monsters and heroes. The snake was a common opponent to champions of civilization, and frequently an outsize variety was a test of courage (for example, for the god Apollo who defeated Pytho, and for Hercules who slaughtered the constantly regenerating Hydra).

2   Perhaps you felt a sense of tragic defeat even though Cato's resolve and attitude to death are heroic. The relentless catalogue of snakes (they just will not lie down!) is viewed as a vehicle for glorifying Cato's Roman Stoicism by Ahl (pp.265–79); he weathers all the terrible trials, physical and mental, that Libya bestows upon him. In contrast, the verses have been called 'disgusting and hilarious'. W.R. Johnson confesses that he 'would be hard pressed to decide which snake takes the cake: each and every one of them is truly wonderful' (Johnson, 1987, p.49). You may have reacted in a similar way as you read through the passage for the first time. It could be argued that Lucan is indulging the Neronian era's taste for 'grotesque absurdities' (p.50), that this is a vivid spectacle for his contemporary reader. For the snake fancying scholar above, however, these vignettes are among the poem's glories, and the scene of the seething sands sustains an immense poetic vitality.

On a more serious note, the *aristeia*[5] of Cato (Ahl, p.259) cannot conceal the ultimate bankruptcy of Stoicism in the face of such an invention of horrors. The fight is unwinnable and unequal; Cato's only triumph is his determination to carry on in spite of so many of his men dying obscenely around him. This is what makes Lucan's Cato an expressionist caricature (Johnson, p.64). 'Cato's soldiers are victims not so much of the monstrous, hilarious snakes as of history and Cato's vainglory' (Johnson, p.56). Perhaps in the light of this interpretation, the snakes symbolize the poisons in the mud of Roman politics and power struggles hatching out in traditional enemy territory. They are irrepressible and – like the Hydra whose heads regrew – in inexhaustible

---

5 A Homeric term for a hero's finest hour when he dispatches numerous enemies on the battlefield.

supply. In contrast, you will be reading about the desert as a place of safety and renewal for the local rebels when you study extracts from Tacitus in the next section (the war against Tacfarinas).

Both Ahl and Johnson consider the whole episode as part of a complex characterization of Cato. I hope you worked out for yourself that Cato is represented by Lucan as stern and incorruptible; Roman writers liked to associate Cato with an earlier republican hero, Regulus, who suffered terrible tortures when he returned to Carthage during the war with Hannibal. Noble Romans still existed, but perhaps the message is that they were fighting against a malaise in the empire that could not be reversed – a gloomy but very Lucan-like moral.

3   As I see it, to substitute snakes for a straightforward battle between Caesar and Cato, and to expressly depict the vipers as fighting in Caesar's place, put the desert of Libya in a clear position of partisanship. In Lucan's epic, it is the actual location of Libya, its wildlife, which is given a malignity towards the Romans. In attacking the Roman republican army under Cato, Libya's desert and its snakes are assisting the irrepressible ambition of Julius Caesar which leaders like Cato challenged. In such a case there is not a straightforward polarity between the destiny of the empire and the foreign opposition.

The North African landscape is allied with the destroyer of the republic, as aider and abetter of Rome's implosion. The treachery of the desert and its denizens take on the time-honoured role of past and present enemies in human form. Ironically, Caesar had made great capital at the time out of the alliance between the African king Juba with Pompey and Cato, and had the two Roman generals declared as *hostes* (enemies) in Rome, depicting them as in service to a foreigner. Lucan's Libyan snakes clarify the issues of republican patriotism versus individual dictatorship. Caesar is the traitor who has been received into the bosom of the African enemy.

From this investigation of some literary uses of Africa and Africans, it is apparent that a distinctively pejorative attitude towards Africa pervaded the pages of Roman authors of the late republic and early empire. This attitude had historical origins in the struggle for domination of the western Mediterranean between Carthage and Rome, but the actual characterizations of Africans and African events are more closely related to the struggles of Roman vices and virtues than to any understanding of

Africa that the authors might have had. Thus Roman social and political problems are projected on to Africa.

This is an appropriate point to turn to Essay Ten, 'The language of dissent'. This essay and the issues and concepts it covers will have a further airing in Block Six. When reading the essay I would like you to focus particularly on the sections entitled 'The rhetoric of resistance' and 'Disarming tactics'. Roman attitudes to rebellious provincials – the chief source used is Tacitus – reveal a number of cultural assumptions, and the essay's literary examples have more than a localized significance.

When you return to the block and interact with the discussion about Tacfarinas in Part Three, you should look out for typically Tacitean techniques in depicting opposition figures. You will be asked to speculate upon Tacfarinas' role as a champion of African 'self-determination', but you should keep in mind his usefulness to Tacitus as a 'model' enemy who can be presented as a sounding board for Roman strengths and weaknesses, ethical, political and military. This 'secondary' exercise should demonstrate to you the complexity of source analysis but also how far you have come in the sophistication of your responses. Please read Essay Ten now.

Part Three: Some cultural observations in the history, literature and art of Africa

BY PHIL PERKINS

3.1 Revolting Africans: reading and interpreting as history Tacitus writing on the rebellions of Tacfarinas

In this section we will be considering an episode from the early history of Roman Africa and looking at how the history, as presented, helps to set the agenda for the interpretation of Roman Africa. You have already studied some of the writings of Tacitus in Blocks One and Four where he was writing about Agricola, Boudicca and Britain. You will be aware of the literary context of Tacitus' writing and also the hazards of taking excerpts of Tacitus out of their context, but his *Annals of Imperial Rome* is the only evidence we have for the revolt of Tacfarinas and so we have to use these extracts if we are investigating dissent against Roman rule in Africa. In the interview about Tacitus with David Braund you listened to in Block Four, it was suggested that Tacitus' descriptions of events were influenced by the themes of each of his books, so here is a brief description of the themes of Books 2, 3 and 4 of the *Annals* from which the Tacfarinas extracts are taken. Book 2 deals with a difficult war against the Germans, treason trials of senators, a war in Armenia and the death of Germanicus, a successful general and member of the imperial family who loyally served Rome. Generally the themes are wars and loyalty to Rome, and the Tacfarinas rebellion fits in with these themes. Book 3 concludes the death of Germanicus and goes on to describe the tension between the senate and the emperor. There is also an account of a rebellion in Gaul. Book 4 largely deals with the development of an autocratic state in Rome and the intimidation of the senatorial classes. The context then is one of wars and rebellions against Rome and the struggle between the senate and the emperor.

Exercise

The revolt led by Tacfarinas was the longest lasting of the many African revolts against Roman domination. While you are reading extract 5.6 in the Supplementary Texts, think about the following questions and take notes to record your responses to the questions for each extract of the text.

1   Who was Tacfarinas and what kinds of things are we told about him?

2   What are we told about the Romans?

3   What do you think Tacitus is most keen to communicate in these passages?

While you are doing this keep our four models of cultural interaction in the back of your mind, and consider whether any of them might fit the historical account. Now read the extracts from Tacitus' *Annals*.

Discussion

These are the notes that I took; yours will differ in detail but the general outline should be similar.

Extract 5.6a:

1   Tacfarinas was a Numidian who had served as a Roman auxiliary (soldier). He was an organizer and leader and managed to get allies. He trained and equipped his troops in the Roman fashion. Tacfarinas was over-optimistic and was defeated in a set-piece battle.

2   The Romans faced the enemy and we are told their battle dispositions. We are told of the renewed military glory of the Furian family and that the Roman commander was given a triumphal parade.

3   Tacitus says that Tacfarinas was organized and the Romans, particularly their commander, were victorious. There is an ominous note at the end where Tacitus says that Furius survived his triumph because of his unassuming life-style. This is a strange remark, and it presumably is a veiled reference to Tiberius' capacity to condemn any senatorial rivals.

Extract 5.6b:

1   Tacfarinas attacks and loots undefended targets and then attacks and destroys a Roman fort.

2   We are told of a Roman defeat and a heroic commander who fought bravely to his death. The new Roman commander brutally punishes his men in an arcane way. This discipline enables the Roman forces to be successful and we hear of more Roman heroics in battle.

3   Tacitus tells of Roman heroism, brutality and discipline. The emperor Tiberius is smeared.

Extract 5.6c:

1   Tacfarinas continued to wage war despite defeats, and also treated Tiberius as if he represented a political force – sending an embassy and demanding land for himself and his people. This proposal was scorned and Tacfarinas branded a bandit. Tacfarinas used guerrilla tactics.

2   The Romans successfully changed their tactics, offering an amnesty, strategically dividing their forces, and building forts and defences. The Romans captured the brother of the rebel leader and withdrew – thinking they were victorious.

3   Tacitus emphasizes the affront caused by the demands of Tacfarinas, and then details the successful strategy and tactics of the Roman senatorial commander.

Extract 5.6d:

1   Tacfarinas continues to plunder Africa, and gathers military support from Mauretania and the Garamantes as well as recruiting the 'destitute and despicable'. Tacfarinas preaches revolution and is portrayed as a freedom fighter. Tacfarinas fights to a heroic death to avoid being taken alive.

2   The Romans fight back and also enlist the military support of Ptolemy (client-king of Mauretania). The Romans launch a successful surprise attack on the camp of Tacfarinas. The Garamantes make peace with Rome, and the king of Mauretania is rewarded for his help.

3   Tacitus puts the blame for the continuing warfare on Tiberius. We are told that Dolabella was not granted a triumph for political reasons.

These extracts are a combination of descriptions of the military events, with a strong emphasis on the Roman victories, and commentary on the political context (in Rome) of the events. But if we think beyond the details contained in the passages, we can consider some of the structural components of the account and look at what the episodes can tell us about Africa, Rome and Tacitus. We can also use the passages to frame further questions about the relationship between Africa and Rome.

Tacfarinas as rebel

These extracts are virtually the only source of information about the revolt of Tacfarinas, but what do they tell us about Tacfarinas? Your notes on question 1 should provide the answer. How does the revolt of Tacfarinas fit in with our four models of cultural interaction? At least in this case we have no difficulty in identifying who is the African and who is the Roman. Much of the evidence suggests model 1, assimilation, was operating. The first extract tells us that Tacfarinas was a Numidian, but also that he had been a Roman soldier, an auxiliary, possibly attached to the Third Legion, which was posted to Africa. The fact that he had been a soldier and deserted suggests that there was a fair degree of co-operation and integration between African and Roman in this period. We are not told what post Tacfarinas held, but he was capable of training his band of 'vagabonds and marauders' in Roman military ways. He was also capable of political organization since he was able to become the chief of the Musulamian people – how he did this and how they were socially or politically organized, we don't know. The alliance with the Mauretanians is further evidence of organizational skills. The forces of Tacfarinas are described as one part armed and trained as Roman troops and the other as light armed raiders: this parallels the Roman organization of a legion and its auxiliaries. This seems to be a striking example of 'Romanization' – Numidians creating a Roman-style army and forming alliances with their neighbours, just as the Roman state did. Perhaps this is why Tacitus records the events of the revolt: the threat was recognizable because it imitated Roman methods and techniques.

At this point in the narrative we have no indication of Tacfarinas' motives for raising and training troops; we are told some joined up to loot and that the troops 'burnt, killed, and intimidated'. This would seem to fit with model 2 of African rejection. In the first paragraph we are told that another tribe joined with 'the rebels'. Precisely how they were rebelling and who they were rebelling against are not explained. Presumably Tacitus is characterizing the raising of arms as a 'rebellion', but what are they actually doing? Did they withdraw co-operation from the Roman state – such as not paying their taxes or complying with the census? We are told they 'burnt, killed, and intimidated', but what did they burn and who did they kill and intimidate? We don't know. We could just assume that the 'rebels' attacked the 'Romans', but we must ask who those 'Romans' were and what form of Roman authority the 'rebels' were challenging. It may be easy enough to ask those questions once we look at the historical narrative in this particular way, but we cannot get an answer from the account of Tacitus, who also has a literary slant to his writings and a political agenda, as you have seen in Blocks One and Four. His is a Roman voice, not an African voice. And what

Tacitus seems most keen to communicate is the military prowess and organization of the Romans, the ins and outs of politics in Rome, and writing an unbalanced biography of Tiberius. He simply is not writing a socio-historical account of the interactions between African and Roman in the early first century AD.

Exercise

So was Tacfarinas 'good' or 'bad'? Before you note down a brief answer, consider the question from two points of view and split it into two questions to answer:

1   Was Tacfarinas a good Roman?

2   Was Tacfarinas a good African?

Discussion

Let us examine the first question. I think the answer must be a pretty clear 'No'. He was first of all a Roman soldier who deserted, so he was a bad Roman as far as the Roman state (or Tacitus) was concerned. Nevertheless, Tacfarinas must have had considerable Roman-style military skills in order to organize his troops and defeat the Romans. Tacfarinas must also be 'bad' because his troops or allies killed, intimidated and burnt properties, creating disorder in a Roman province. Was there anything 'good' about Tacfarinas? If there was, Tacitus does not communicate it. So, seen from the centre in Rome Tacfarinas was a thoroughly bad thing.

But what impression can be created by rephrasing our question as 'Was Tacfarinas a good African?' He organized the Africans and gave various tribes and peoples some form of political cohesion and motivated them to fight together against the Roman legions. Whether this was a 'good' thing is debatable: increasing political sophistication is generally considered good, but in this case it also engendered a long war against Roman power. We are only really given one insight into the motivation of the Africans: Tacfarinas characterized his supporters as those who 'preferred freedom to slavery'. So perhaps we might consider Tacfarinas as a 'good' African if he is fighting against slavery, but we don't know if his words, communicated by Tacitus, are meant to be literal – suggesting that Romans were making Africans into slaves – or metaphorical – suggesting that some previous and better state of freedom, now lost, had once existed. You have already met the concept of a 'freedom fighter' with Boudicca on audio cassette 4. The theme of 'freedom' might also be related to Tacitus' account of the struggle between the senators and the autocratic emperor, and so be part of Tacitus' own agenda. Perhaps unsurprisingly, the answer to 'was Tacfarinas "good" or "bad"?' is that it rather depends on how you choose to define 'good' and 'bad' and also from whose viewpoint you are looking at the question.

3.2   Economic power and exchange

One way to approach the issue of whether Africa's period as a Roman province was a positive or negative episode is to consider the economic history of Africa. The study of the economy of Africa forms part of the contextualization of your study of culture. This section will concentrate upon the identification and interpretation of economic activity in Africa as well as its relation, as a province, to the city of Rome at the centre of the empire. In this way a second level of investigation is added to the binary opposition of Africa and Rome: that of centre and periphery. We will consider the economic relationship as a manifestation of power and the question of economic development and exploitation of one party by the other.

To investigate this topic, now do the following activities (as you work through them, be thinking about the power of Rome to exploit the province of Africa):

1   Watch the video sequence, 'Economic power and exchange: Africa and Rome' (video cassette 3, t.c. 28:08–49:40).

2   Read the extracts (and their introductions) in Lewis and Reinhold on:

- grain production in Africa (pp.84–5);
- imperial estates in Africa (pp.95–9);
- taxation remission (pp.400–1);
- *annona* (pp.61–4);
- the grain fleet and privileges for shipowners (pp.112–17);
- agencies (pp.109–11).

3   Re-read pp.197–9 ('Managed production and consumption') and pp.209–11 (from 'In the case of southern Spain, ...') of Essay Seven, 'Power, culture and identity in the Roman economy'.

Parts of Africa, especially the Mejerda Valley, are extremely fertile, and this is attested by the vast shipments of grain which were extracted from Africa in the form of tax or produce and shipped to Italy to feed the people of Rome. The province also produced large quantities of olives and olive oil (a good source of protein and fat as well as lighting) and fish products such as sauces. As you saw on the video, evidence for this exportation may be seen in Monte Testaccio in Rome, where some 25 per cent of the amphorae are African in origin. The exchange, particularly of oil, became even more intensive with time, and through the third, fourth and fifth centuries Africa and Tripolitania supplied much of the basin of the western Mediterranean with oil. African amphorae are a common site find throughout this period and region. In the text extracts and the video you have seen some of the details of the infrastructure and organization of this exchange, some of the legal controls and taxation issues. There is still much more to be discovered about the who, how, when and why of this exchange, but we can begin to reach some preliminary conclusions by asking some general questions.

First, was Rome, particularly the city of Rome and the Roman state, economically exploiting the province of Africa? In as much as taxes in money or kind were extracted from the province, then Africa can be seen as exporting a proportion of its wealth and income to the imperial administration in Rome. However, most of the Roman empire was in a similar position. There were tax-free areas, such as the city of Thugga or Italy, and there were occasional exemptions, but generally taxes needed to be paid on a regular basis. Whether or not the taxes were exploitative rather depends upon their levels and also what the people of the province received in return. The imperial government provided for justice in the provincial capital and also provided for security in the form of the Third Legion, which was based first in Africa but progressively further into Numidia and Mauretania as Roman military control extended towards the desert areas (see Figure 5.8). Imperial patronage, although not necessarily directly related to taxes, could also be important in some communities, providing them with amenities and facilities such as baths, theatres and amphitheatres. At a deeper level, the demands made upon the productivity of Africa can also be seen as stimulating production, providing for nutritional needs as well as the need to pay taxes. A tax in kind on grain, for example, encourages a level of grain production above subsistence, and production above subsistence levels provides a cushion against famine. The development of the *annona* route as an axis of exchange can also be seen as stimulating the transportation and production of other produce. For example, the olive oil followed the route of the grain, as did much of the African Red Slip ware. The city of Rome also acted as a market for the surplus production of the province, and so the existence of trade routes between the province and Rome generated a flow of wealth back into the province. To some extent the centre in Rome and the province on the southern shore of the Mediterranean became economically interdependent.

Figure 5.8 *General view of the excavated city founded in* AD *97 for veterans of the Third Legion, Djemila, Algeria. DAI neg. no.64.1653. (Photo: Sichtermann/German Archaeological Institute, Rome)*

Is it possible to suggest that this economic interdependence was a positive or negative force? Once again it depends upon the definitions and perspectives adopted. No doubt for a large section of the population the mechanisms of the Roman empire did little to enhance their status or conditions, which were close to subsistence. The vicissitudes of the weather and seasons probably had more influence upon their well-being than the efficiency of the tax collector. On the other hand, the Roman period saw a great increase in the density of urban settlement in Africa. Many of these towns and cities were well equipped with public buildings, and even if some were for entertainment and social interaction (theatres) rather than subsistence (markets), others such as baths and aqueducts may well have had a significant impact on public health and so increased life expectancy. For higher-status individuals the connection to the city of Rome provided opportunities for both wealth generation through trade and also status enhancement through participating in local and provincial politics, and ultimately metropolitan politics in Rome. Thus seen from the point of view of urban development and economic activity, some of Africa flourished under Roman power.

3.3   The rhetoric of praise

If we move from economic foundations to a literary expression of African sentiments, we can explore a further element of cultural development in Africa. Although some of the individual figures in Roman literature had provincial backgrounds, most worked in Rome and did not express provincial sentiments in any way that we might be able to recognize as a vernacular tradition opposed to a mainstream Roman tradition. However, one author, Apuleius, who was born in the early second century at Madaura in Africa, described himself as half-Numidian, half-Gaetulian (that is, from the tribe of the Gaetules in the Atlas Mountains of north-west Africa). His father was a *duumvir* and he wrote in Latin. He is best known for *The Golden Ass*, a magical story of the adventures of a man turned into an ass; you have already read an extract in Block Three, where he describes a procession for an Egyptian goddess in an Asian city, Cenchreae.

Exercise

The extract you will study comes from a collection of short fragments of writing known collectively as the *Florida*. These are generally short pieces of writing taken from public speeches of Apuleius. This piece is a combination of intellectual pomposity (and verbosity) combined with praise (panegyric) to the city of Carthage, where the speech may have been delivered. Above all, Apuleius seems keen to emphasize his own learning. Read extract 5.7 now, referring to the footnotes (which explain the obscure classical references). As you read, note down the cultural influences you see acting on Apuleius' work.

Discussion

Apuleius starts with a dinner party quip and adapts the theme to the acquisition of knowledge, associating each drink to the gathering of more knowledge. However, we should note that Apuleius' divisions of knowledge do not precisely match the traditional divisions generally attributed to each of the nine Greek Muses; whether this is a feature of the oratory or a product of Apuleius' own education is a matter for speculation. He also equates his thirst for knowledge with drinking the fourth cup – for madness – and doesn't forget to tell us that he was educated at Athens. He boasts he can write verses, dialogues, hymns, modulations, histories and satires. He then has a timely attack of modesty, and claims that even if he has no great capacity for learning then at least the attempt is worthwhile. However, no degree of learning can earn as much praise as giving a good speech at Carthage, a city which is a centre of learning, an inspiration for Africa and nurturer of toga wearers.

So what can we see of Afro-Roman culture and identity in this highly stylized and convoluted passage? Apuleius makes much of his learning of Greek culture, very much following the fashion of the Second Sophistic (which you have studied in Block Three, Part Two); there is no mention of African or Roman scholars he may have studied. What is implicit in the scenario Apuleius sets up is the fact that he is an African speaking in Latin in the provincial capital of Roman Africa to an educated audience and alluding to an intellectual world which has its roots in classical Greece, even though his first language was Punic. This city is then set up as an exemplar to the remainder of Africa, which presumably should aspire to the level of education witnessed in Carthage. In the final line there is an allusion to Roman culture with mention of the Carmena, an obscure set of fountain nymphs, one of whom, Egeria, was the spirit of the sacred fountain used by the Vestal Virgins. One of their functions was to watch over childbirth, and presumably it is this role which is referred to for Carthage, watching over the birth of toga-wearing citizens of the Roman city of Carthage. In summary, the piece is a mixture of Greek intellectual references set in an African city with some references to Roman symbolism.

Apuleius is not setting up a confrontation between African and Roman, but rather highlighting access to a Greek cultural education as a praiseworthy aspect of the city of Carthage. This is neatly paralleled in the Greek mottos and themes you saw in the mosaics of élite flooring in Bulla Regia and Thugga. Apuleius is not promoting a Roman intellectual culture, nor is he recognizing a distinctive African intellectual culture. It would seem that the opposition we have been investigating between the African and the Roman is not one that Apuleius perceived in the intellectual life of Carthage.

3.4   Afro-Roman art

The votive stone illustrated on the left in Plate 5.9 (and shown on video cassette 3, t.c.16:18–58) was found at Maghrawa near Mactar, not far from Thugga, in central Tunisia. It has been dated to the last quarter of the first century AD (Bisi, 1978; M'charek, 1988). The stone is one of a small group of similar monuments from the area now scattered between the museums of Europe and Tunisia. It is inscribed at the bottom with BELLIC ❤ MAX / F ❤ V ❤ S ❤ L ❤ A ❤ S. The meaning of this inscription is not certain because of the abbreviations, but it is in Latin and probably reads 'Bellicus son of Maximus fulfilled his vow with a willing spirit'. The stone therefore commemorates and fulfills a vow made to the gods by Bellicus.

The monument displays a combination of African and Roman motifs and traits. The general form of the stone, a tall pillar with a pointed top, is in the tradition of Punic tombstones which date back to at least the third century BC (see Plate 5.10). The representation of columns or even a small building on tombs is also a frequent Punic motif; the building on this stone is apparently a classical structure, a temple (or *aedicule*) with a pediment and crude Corinthian capitals. The portrait of the man who set up the dedication, sitting inside the temple and wearing a toga, is a Roman-style representation. He is holding a scroll, a symbol of knowledge. Looking carefully at the temple structure, it becomes apparent that there is something untypical about it: the podium and columns are Roman enough but above them, where the architrave should be, is a panel of coffering (seen here as two rows of squares). This kind of coffering was commonly used in the ceiling of the porticoes of classical temples (such as the temple of Mars Ultor in the Forum of Augustus at Rome or the monumental temple of Serapis at Ephesus). In this case the coffering creates a very unperspectival representation of a temple façade in which the columns are represented front-on and the ceiling is seen from underneath. Above the coffering is an architrave and a pediment containing a female head. So we have a classical building depicted in a non-classical representation. Below the temple is the inscription, which – despite being in Latin – reproduces the traditional African form of naming: 'Bellicus son of Maximus'.

There is further interest in the top part of the stone where there is a hierarchical representation of gods along with their attributes and symbols of nature, fertility and the cosmos. At the top is a male figure clutching a thunder bolt. This is Baal Hammon, Punic god of the sun (among other things), and a sun is represented below to the right, but it is also the image of Jupiter the thunderer and god of the heavens, and stars are represented on either side of the crescent moon beneath him. Below is another figure with a roughly triangular body mimicking the shape of the 'sign of Tanit',[6] a motif representing the Phoenician goddess Tanit, who became the goddess Juno Caelestis in the Roman period. She was the queen of the heavens, the new moon and birth (among other things), and is represented holding symbols of fecundity, a cornucopia (horn of plenty) from which hangs a bunch of grapes and a pomegranate. Above her head is a crescent moon (from which the Baal figures rises), and below some flowers to the left and right are her sacred birds, doves. Below these and standing on the pediment of the temple are, on the left, the figure of Dionysus (or Liber) holding a *cantharus* (a drinking cup) and, on the right, a naked Venus, both divinities of fertility and both represented in distinctly unclassical form even if they have classical attributes. The figures do not seem to form a narrative, but take their places in the pantheon of Olympian and Punic deities above the temple.

Overall the monument is a juxtaposition of Punic and Roman forms and deities all combining on the stone. Although many of the objects depicted are familiar from Roman art, their representation here takes on a distinctly unclassical aspect. If such monuments are held up against the most classical of Roman art, they might be seen as deficient in some ways. So, for example, if we compare it with another sacred monument, an altar to the *gens Augusta* from Carthage (Plate 5.11), a number of points can be made.

The style of the reliefs here is similar to major Augustan monuments such as the Ara Pacis in Rome (Colour Plate 1.1). The altar has a typical Roman shape, and on one side depicts a literary text, a scene from the *Aeneid* (2.707–11) where Aeneas flees from Troy taking his father, son and gods with him, a quintessential Roman act of piety and duty. The scene is represented as part of a classical narrative, with the figures carefully laid out proceeding from right to left. The figures are shown in three-quarters profile, and although in low relief are well rounded and moulded. On the second side is a scene of a bull sacrifice; on the third an image of the Greek god Apollo with lyre, tripod and griffon; and on the fourth a personification of Roma seated on a pile of weapons and holding a small figure of the goddess Victory; in front of her is an altar bearing a globe and a cornucopia. In summary, the altar from Carthage is very classical both in content and in style.

In contrast, the votive stone mixes up classical and Punic divinities, there is no narrative, the figures face forward and are very flat and not at all naturalistic. If we judge it as a piece of classical Roman art, it is very poor and crude indeed. How are we to interpret this difference?

6

The person who carved the votive stone might be said not to understand, or be able to represent, the rules of classical perspective and so failed to 'accurately' represent the classical architecture of the temple or *aedicule*. The artist who carved the altar was working within the conventions of Roman art by representing a well-known scene from legend in a recognized form of a naturalistic narrative frieze. In contrast, the divinities on the votive stone do not reproduce the familiar models of Graeco-Roman religion, even if they carry some of their attributes and meanings.

The difference in the end is that the altar and the votive stone belong to different cultural contexts where the form and style of representation differed. They also address a different audience. The altar is a public monument to the ruling family of the imperial power at Rome, and as such carries with it political and cultural messages which help to create and reinforce the identity of 'Roman' and the impact of Roman power in Carthage, the provincial capital. The votive stone, on the other hand, is both a private and public monument. It is a memorial to the vow and dedication made by an individual, a public statement of his identity through his image, his title and the representation of some of his world of beliefs in the form of the divine hierarchy and fertility themes represented on his stone. Those who would have seen the stone were probably local people who would have shared his beliefs and understood the same visual language of representation and symbolism.

If this difference is recognized and the comparison with classical art is not made in terms of 'good' art compared with 'bad' art, then we can see the votive stone as a valid expression of an art which, although representing some classical elements, does not adopt a purely classical form to represent them. Such works of art are often described as 'rustic', 'decadent', 'debased' or 'provincial'; they are frequently held to be inferior to the 'best of' classical art to be found in metropolitan centres. This form of description sets such works apart, suggesting that they do not really belong in the category of canonical classical art. Such distinctions end up perpetuating a scenario where 'good = Roman' and 'bad = indigenous'. We can progress our understanding by discarding such divisions and accepting art like the votive stone as a valid expression of the art that was produced in the province of Africa, and including it, along with the Augustan altar, as part of the body of Romano-African art which has survived. It is also a potent representation of the fusion of Roman and African forms of representation and belief.

Part Four: Becoming aware of how we are studying the past

BY PHIL PERKINS

4.1 Figures in a landscape: modern authors and North Africa

An important aspect of studying the past is being aware of the history of past studies of history. This is known as historiography, and a study of the history of history can provide insights into how we got to know what we know about the past. It can also inform us about how recent cultural contexts have shaped the questions we have asked about the past and influenced our understanding. The same study of the development of ideas about the past can also be applied to broader cultural history, archaeology and literary studies. In this part of the block we will begin to consider these questions with reference to the recent history of North Africa using the Offprints Book and audio cassette 4.

Your first activity is to read an article by David Mattingly, 'From one colonialism to another: imperialism and the Maghreb' (offprint 5.1). The article considers the history of archaeological activity in North Africa, particularly by French and Italian researchers. For this reason it contains some quotations in French or Italian, which are translated for you after the offprint along with a commentary upon some of the specialist terms he uses. Please read offprint 5.1 now, and as you read take notes on the factors which have influenced research into Roman Africa.

David Mattingly is an archaeologist and so his comments and writing apply to that area of study, but a similar discussion and critique could be made about other areas of cultural history, such as political history, art history or literature. In the light of David Mattingly's views on the history of the study of Roman North Africa and the comments he makes about colonialist and imperialist constructions of the past, perhaps we should critically revise how and what we have been studying in the block so far. You may like to open the texts and look back at your notes as I discuss the block and set books.

First of all, let us look back at the extract from Goodman which you read at the start of the block with new-found colonialist and imperialist sensibilities. The first sentence in Goodman on page 276 clearly puts Africa in the position of 'colony': 'By 44 BC the whole of the North African coastline already lay within the Roman sphere of influence, and in general, from the viewpoint of the Roman state, the region remained untroublesome for the next three centuries, whether by the co-operation or the suppression of the natives.' There then follows a brief account of pre-Roman North Africa, much of it framed by reference to non-African civilizations of Phoenicia, Greece and Rome. There is then a long section (pp.277–81) on the military conquests and exploits of the imperialist colonizing power. It is a catalogue of African defeats and Roman victories, and even includes the assertion by Pliny that an African tribe ate dog food! Oh dear! The final long section concentrates upon 'urbanization', itself a value-laden term: why not call it 'de-ruralization' or 'destruction of indigenous settlement patterns by Roman militaristic invaders' instead? On page 281 Goodman suggests that there was extensive emigration from Italy to Africa. Mattingly has suggested there is little evidence for this; however, immigration was one of the key elements of colonization and emigration from Italy was a major phenomenon in the earlier part of the twentieth century, not only to Africa but also to the Americas and other parts of Europe. So is recent history being strongly reflected upon Roman history here? We are then told how Roman-style settlements were built and how the indigenous people were organized into 'manageable administrative units'. (I think they were called 'reservations' in the 'Wild West'.) On pages 282–3 we see colonialist emperors owning large tracts of land and patronizing the natives. On page 283 we learn that a few natives did manage to practise Roman culture, but on the next page we discover that some low-status Africans survived to be policed by the Roman military. Finally we discover that the imperialist's language, Latin, was used for inscriptions, but that the indigenous language survived, as did some religious cults. The final sentence repeats the Christian Tertullian's assertion that public child sacrifice was practised in the native cult of Saturn. Oh dear! How awful could the natives possibly be?

This critique has been deliberately searing or ironic in places and also somewhat unfair, but it does show how Goodman's brief summary can be clearly seen as derived from colonialist and imperialist views of African history, as well as dwelling upon alleged unnatural acts by Africans. The critique is not intended to imply that the history written by Goodman is worthless and that you wasted your time reading it at the beginning of the block. Goodman's account follows in the well-established tradition of what constitutes traditional Roman history, and it is a valid account of that history. But at this stage in the course we are trying to push at the limits of traditional history and broaden our cultural understanding of ancient history.

Well, let us now see how Wells fares between pages 224 and 233. First, Wells sets the scene describing the location of an ancient Roman town at Tiddis, even making reference to the modern landscape. The pre-Roman origins of the city are mentioned, and then we hear about the benefits that being colonized by Rome brought to the town: an arch and gates, inscriptions, paved streets, a foreign cult, cisterns, a market, a forum, temples to Roman gods (with a bit of imagination), imperial statues, an inscription to a patron (and probably native) of the town who achieved high status in the Roman military regime and later went on to introduce the inhabitants of southern Scotland to the benefits of empire. All these things are held to indicate that the inhabitants of the town were 'happy and prosperous'. It seems that all of these Roman-style 'facilities' are unquestionably an improvement on what went before. We then hear at length (pp. 226–9) how Roman-style agriculture was introduced to Africa and much of its produce was taxed as *annona*. This leads to discussion of some minor manufacturing, and then to the city of Carthage where 'the acropolis of Punic Carthage, had been levelled in Augustus's day' (p.230) (see Plate 5.12). This seems to be a minimization of a deliberate piece of cultural cleansing with the removal of the historic centre of ancient Carthage and its replacement with the official buildings of a Roman provincial capital and planned residential areas (see Figure 5.7, p.32).

On page 231 we learn about how the marble quarry at Chemtou was exploited to embellish the imperial capital. We are then told how the Roman military had to suppress some natives, and finally an anecdote about how the efficient imperial military forces succeeded in completing a defective aqueduct.

So Wells's account of Africa (which does not claim to be a systematic summary) concentrates on the benefits of the Roman style of city and what an African family might achieve within the military system of the Roman empire. This has colonialist undertones in that it concentrates on Roman improvements and military matters, but seems to be more sympathetic to the African elements than Goodman. The motives and impact of Roman domination on Carthage seem to be under-emphasized, and the economic exploitation of the province is not deeply investigated.

Now turning a critical eye to the Block Five materials and moving on to the video and discussion of Thugga, the exercise and argument revolve around contrasting the elements which can be seen to be Roman and those which are African. This might seem to be a reasonable approach to take, in that it is designed to tease out issues of culture, identity and power. However, by setting up the opposition of Roman and African, the discussion is immediately falling into a colonialist and imperialist model by attempting to identify one social, political and cultural block as Roman (the imperial power) and another as African (the colonized subject). Indeed the four models for possible cultural interaction – assimilation, rejection, separation or fusion – are themselves operating within the framework of conqueror and conquered, dominant and dominated culture. The models of separation or fusion are perhaps less rooted in such a framework because they do not require either cultural tradition to dominate. The fourth model allows for the emergence of something new from a contact between two different cultures. The studies that follow all investigate various possibilities of identifying the African or the Roman in the cultural record, and so are also operating within a colonial context with a projecting culture (Roman) and a receiving culture (African). Nevertheless, the exercise of polarizing the issues into a confrontation of Roman and African has helped to clarify both what we think of as Roman and what we think of as African, and our four models have helped us to think about what happens when different cultures come into contact.

Following this, an African identity which is independent of the modern colonial model is investigated. Reading the literary images of Africa and Africans, we can see that the Romans had their own set of steroetypes and preconceived notions of what Africa and its inhabitants were like. The case of Tacitus' account of Tacfarinas' rebellion is slightly different in that it begins to consider more how a Roman colonialist and Roman imperialist version of history was constructed by Tacitus. The fact that it is now the only surviving narrative of these historical events means that it inevitably shapes our perceptions of the episode and presents events from the Roman point of view. But in this case it projects a Roman imperialistic view rather than a modern one. However, our modern imperialist version of the history derives from the Roman imperialist sources.

Building on the previous studies, the next sections attempted to evaluate positive and negative aspects of the relationship between Rome and Africa. The first considered the economic base and economic relationships between Africa and Rome, and so explicitly addressed questions of imperialist economic exploitation, but without leaving the framework of the division between Rome the colonizing power and Africa the colonized province. The final literary study of the Apuleius speech attempted to impose the African versus Roman model, but ran into trouble because the supposed binary opposition could not really be found; instead there was a celebration of a completely different form of intellectual culture, Hellenism. This perhaps takes us away from the colonial discourse and introduces another element into the cultural history of Africa as part of a wider Mediterranean world system. However, Hellenism has itself to be seen as the adopted culture of the imperialist Roman power rather than an independent and benign cultural force from Greece, even if Africa had been exposed to Hellenistic cultural influences before the Roman conquest (think of the monument on the hill of Saturn at Chemtou on video cassette 3,

'Economic power and exchange' sequence). The final study considered a votive stone which can be seen as a fusion of Roman and African elements, and asked how we might evaluate it when it is compared with art where classical influences are stronger and more visible. Here the 'colonizing' Roman art is explicitly contrasted with the 'colonized' indigenous art.

4.2 Do not consume the packaging

So far imperialist and colonialist ideas and thinking have been presented as undesirable, although this opinion has not been discussed in detail. It's all very well to wring our hands about poor Punic farmers being oppressed by the Roman military, but surely things like good government and adequate clean water supplies did improve material conditions for the people living in North Africa (this seems to be Wells's view). And surely the Roman state actually was imperialistic and colonizing; there is plenty of evidence for that and you have already studied some of it. The imperialistic and colonizing features of the Roman empire cannot be denied, and they form one of the major areas of study in contemporary Roman studies. However, a separation needs to be maintained between the object of study – in this case Roman imperialism and colonialism – and how we study it. We need to keep a perspective that allows us to remember that Roman imperialism and colonialism were not the same as modern imperialism and colonialism. Furthermore, ideas developed in a colonial and imperial context cannot avoid being influenced by that context, be it from the viewpoint of French or Italian colonizers in North Africa or from the viewpoint of Britain with the history behind it of the collapse of the British empire and the emergence of post-colonial states in much of the world during the twentieth century. Other interpretations and histories coming from different cultural backgrounds and viewpoints can also be written. As discussed by Mattingly, one response from North Africa to this situation has been to develop explanations which emphasize the positive aspects of African culture and denigrate the benefits of empire.

Exercise

Read the introduction to a history of Roman Africa provided in extract 5.8. Note down the topics that Mahjoubi has chosen to discuss.

Discussion

Let us now examine this anti-colonialist text. The start is explicit enough; where another text might have started, 'After the *conquest* of Carthage in −146 and the *elevation* of her territory to the status of a Roman province', the choice of words begins to set the agenda. The text then goes on to suggest that more study of Numidian history is needed, which is certainly true. The last sentence of the first paragraph suggests that there is a sharp periodization of North African history and both a clear beginning and a clear end to the Roman period in Africa. The text then goes on to stress that Roman military conquest and the 'pacification' were not easy and that eventually the domination of Rome was undermined by military resistance (there were later rebels to follow in the footsteps of Tacfarinas). The Roman origin of historical sources and the colonial stance of recent historiography are also noted.

This account sets the scene for a description of Roman Africa which de-emphasizes Roman 'achievements' and values the African contribution. However, we have to see it as a product of the post-colonial era, and much of its discussion is just as rooted in the colonially based (and indeed historically rooted) division between the Roman and the African as most of the other accounts we have encountered. The account replaces the triumphalism of the colonial power with a heroic nationalist fight for freedom from Roman oppressors.

4.3   Conclusion: a way forward

Now listen to an audio interview with David Mattingly, 'From one colonialism to another', where he discusses his article which you read earlier and various approaches to studying Roman Africa (audio cassette 4, band 3).

So what can we do to escape from the shackles of a colonialist and imperialist view of Africa in the Roman period? A first approach is to think carefully about the characterizations of Roman and African we have been studying so far. Neither of these was monolithic and fixed in time. By now you have learned that the Roman empire was incredibly diverse, and there is a great deal of variation between Italy (Block Two), Greece and Asia Minor (Block Three), Britain (Block Four) and Africa (Block Five), even though there are visible similarities. But just like 'Rome', 'Africa' was not monolithic. This block has been using the word 'African' in a loose way so far in order to oppose it with 'Roman' (which is why the discussion of the term 'Africa' at the start of the block was rather limited). Strictly, the term referred to the Roman province of Africa, but even this changed though time: Africa Vetus (Old Africa), the area around Carthage, was extended by Julius Caesar to include parts of Numidia creating Africa Novus (New Africa). Later this area was Africa Proconsularis (Africa administered by a proconsul) and later still split into Zeugitania and Byzacena. To the east were the provinces of Tripolitania and Cyrenaica (modern Libya) and then Egypt, and to the west Numidia, Mauretania Caesariensis (largely northern Algeria) and Mauretania Tingitana (largely northern Morocco). This block has only considered evidence from a limited area of Africa Proconsularis; other neighbouring areas, whose histories and cultures were closely related, have been ignored. The term Africa is often used to include all of these areas and create some sense of unity between them. However, when they are studied in detail, differences appear between their cultures and histories. Cyrenaica was deeply influenced by the Greek world, Egypt had its own ancient cultural heritage, and Mauretania Tingitana had close contact with Spain. Even within Africa Proconsularis differences can be identified between different areas; thus mosaics from Carthage and the north can be seen to differ from those further south from Sousse (Figure 5.4) or El Djem where, for example, interwoven garland frames and large figured scenes are more common. Moving further away to southern Numidia a mosaic from Timgad (see Plate 5.13) is stylistically different from anything in Africa Proconsularis. So the closer one looks, the more the monolithic concept of 'Africa' diminishes. This suggests that we should be careful when characterizing something as African and remember that it might not be generalizable to the whole of Africa. So if we de-polarize what we are studying and treat 'Roman' and 'African' as limited generalizing terms, we can consider all our evidence as 'Romano-African' (or Afro-Roman) and compare it with other cultural combinations from other parts of the empire and beyond.

Furthermore, even if we can see some things as 'African' or 'Roman', or Roman culture itself stereotyped 'Roman' and 'African', the different identities and cultural expressions which are summed up as 'African-ness' and 'Roman-ness' formed a part of the common experience of those living in the province. So 'African-ness' and 'Roman-ness' formed a territory for negotiation in which individuals constructed their own cultural identities. Apuleius is an example of this negotiation: he expresses his African descent and tribal identity but practises and preaches Graeco-Roman culture. These observations need not be limited to 'African' and 'Roman' cultures, but could be extended to other cultural identities in the classical world such as 'Greek' culture or 'barbarian' culture.

A second point to insist upon is that judgements about the quality or value of particular forms of evidence should be resisted. So an 'indigenous' sculpture and a 'Roman' sculpture should be considered as having equal potential as a source of evidence. They may not address the same issues, but that does not necessarily mean that one is more or less important.

David Mattingly also suggested that advances can be made by studying new topics of interest such as the economy and skeletal evidence rather than focusing on traditional areas such as literature, history or art. In this block you have studied a diverse range of evidence, some traditional and some more novel, but it is important to keep a breadth of study and to see how different sources can provide differing and complementary evidence for our field of study. This breadth of areas of study provides one context for our particular study of Africa, and David Mattingly points out another at the end of the interview where he suggests that consideration of a long time scale (often referred to in French as the *longue durée*) helps to place Roman Africa in a continuum of development from Punic Africa through Roman Africa and on into Islamic Africa. This course focuses on a short period of the early Roman empire, but we have at least studied some of the earlier context of Punic Africa even if we have not gone on to study later Roman (see, for example, Colour Plate 5.8) and Islamic Africa.

It is always important to be aware of the contexts and origins of the ideas we are using in developing an understanding of the past. So an interpretation from a colonialist viewpoint might well be useful, but it also needs to be understood as only one account of a situation from the past which has been written by an author coming from a particular cultural experience. Other ideas and viewpoints rooted in different cultures can also be valid and need to be considered and taken into account. Thus the account by Mahjoubi given in extract 5.8 is not simply 'wrong' or just 'different' to 'traditional' accounts such as those by Wells or Goodman: it is a parallel account of the same history written from a different cultural viewpoint. The challenge that faces us is to be able to study the distant past with an awareness of our own cultural background and with an openness to other interpretations derived from different experiences of that same past. And this is why we have been talking throughout about the city of Thugga – its ancient name – rather than the more commonly used Dougga, which is a Frenchified version of the name given to the site by the French colonial power. Awareness of the past continues to have a political dimension and even names carry historical baggage with them: as this block was being prepared, the name of Chemtou (Frenchified) has been officially changed to Chimtou (Berber style), which might lead to confusion but at least sounds nearer to the ancient Simitthus.

In Block Six you will be studying a part of the world which has a deep and rich history. It has also been, and still is, the scene of much conflict and political and cultural strife. Block Six may not explicitly identify the themes which you have studied in this block, but as you study look out for them and use the skills you have developed here to keep a critical eye on the sources, both primary and secondary, and the contexts of the study.

Key dates

References

AHL, F.M. (1976) *Lucan: an Introduction*, Ithaca and London, Cornell University Press.

BISI, A.M. (1978) 'A proposito di alcune stele del tipo della Ghorfa al British Museum', *Antiquités Africaines*, 12, pp.21–88.

DUNCAN-JONES, R. (1990) *Structure and Scale in the Roman Economy*, Cambridge, Cambridge University Press.

GOULD, H.E. and WHITELEY, J.L. (eds) (1947) *P. Vergilius Maro: Aeneid, Book One*, London, Macmillan.

JACQUES, F. (1989) 'L'urbanisme en Italie et en Afrique romaines', *Journal of Roman Archaeology*, 2, pp.238–44.

JOHNSON, W.R. (1987) *Momentary Monsters: Lucan and his Heroes*, Ithaca and London, Cornell University Press.

M'CHAREK, A. (1988) 'Maghrawa, lieu de provenence des stèles punico-numide dites de la Ghorfa', *Melanges de l'École Français de Rome Antiquité*, 100, 2, pp.731–61.

Further reading

The following books are not part of the course materials. You are not expected to obtain, read or study these items. However, if you would like to find out more about some of the topics presented in the block, you may find the following list a useful starting point.

BRETT, M. and FENTRESS, E. (1996) *The Berbers*, Oxford, Blackwell.

LANCEL, S. (1995) *Carthage: a History*, Oxford, Blackwell.

MATTINGLY, D.J. (1995) *Tripolitania*, London, Batsford.

MATTINGLY, D.J. and HITCHNER, R.B. (1995) 'Roman Africa: an archaeological survey', *Journal of Roman Studies*, vol.LXXXV, pp.165–213.

RAVEN, S. (1993) *Rome in Africa*, London and New York, Routledge.

SAID, E.W. (1993) *Culture and Imperialism*, London, Chatto and Windus.